A SELF PORTRAIT

Select the brush stroke, the canvas, the colors.
Your lip may quiver, but
Your stance is firm.

Paint concentric circles
Ask yourself again
What do I need?…I want?

It's revolutionary to listen
To your inner child.
To yourself.

Give the subject
Hours of study.
It's a life's work.

B. JOAN HICKEY, 1991

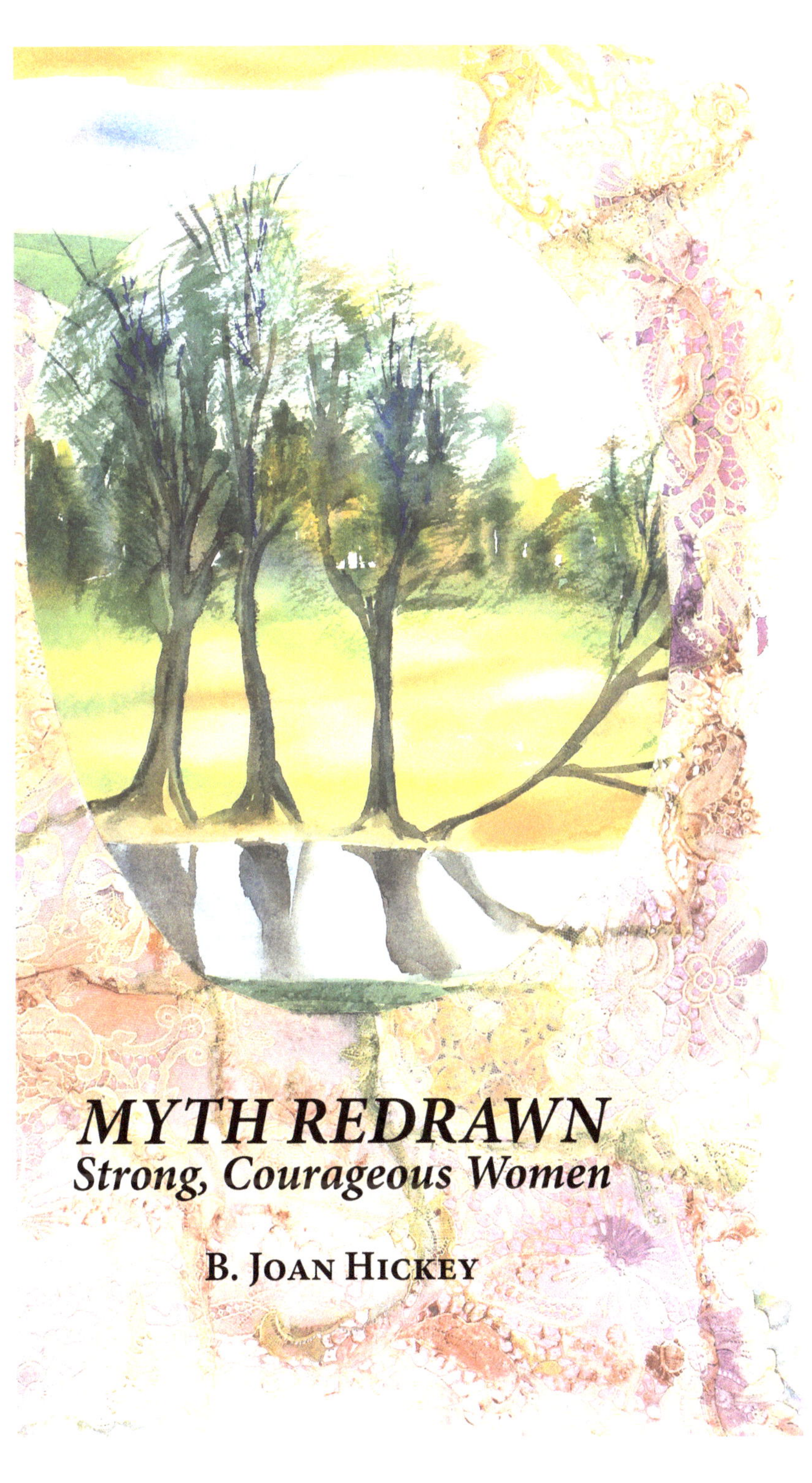
MYTH REDRAWN
Strong, Courageous Women
B. JOAN HICKEY

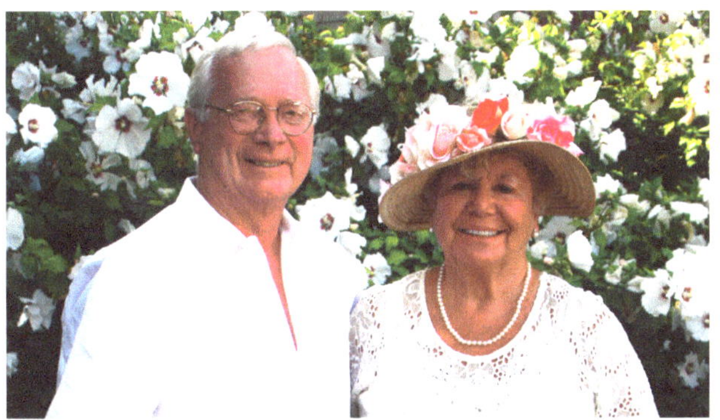

Ode To Dennis F. Hickey

Dennis has been my love, my guide, and my collaborator since I met him in 1968. We have successfully blended the needs of parallel careers and lives. We daily have time to share a great glass of wine and the sunset.

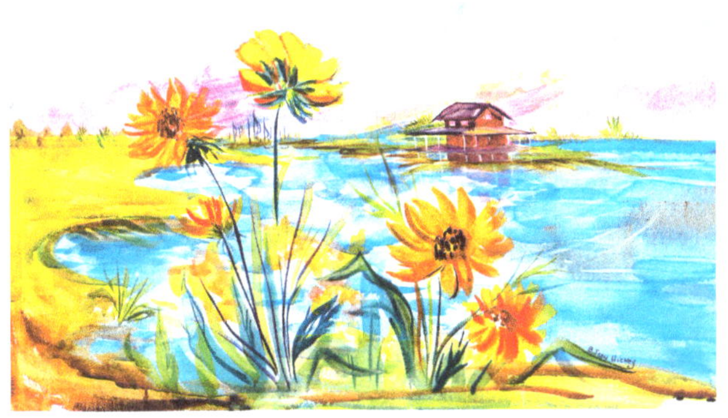

Dedication

For my grandmothers, Jenny V. Webster, May Day,
Delia Dunn-Hussey, my mother Lucilla "Coey" Hussey,
my beloved husband, Dennis F. Hickey, my son,
Jeffrey L. Hickey and his wife, Hannah Lintner-Hickey,
and our precious granddaughter Riley J. Hickey.

(Autumn Joy, 2015, 28"w x 20"h, original watercolor by B. Joan Hickey)

TABLE OF CONTENTS

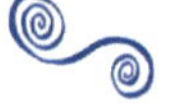

ACKNOWLEDGEMENTS

I sincerely thank my artist mentors M.I. Cake, collage, Joan Downey, artist mentor, Laura Lyons, fiber artist/shepherd, Jennifer Davies, fiber artist, Dalton Patton, photographer and technical assistant, Jen Payne, graphic design and technical assistance, Dr. Margaret D. Lindsey formerly of the Graduate Liberal studies, Wesleyan University, my sister, artist mentor Hawley J. Hussey, my beloved husband Dennis Hickey, and all my friends, artist mentors, and the "doers" who continue to contribute to this effort.

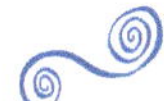

PREFACE

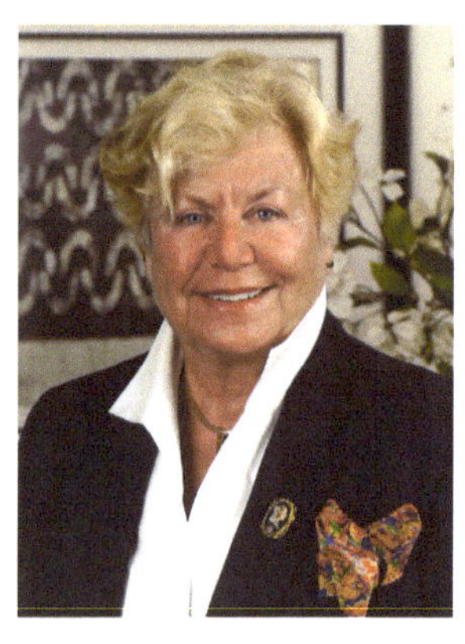

B. Joan Hickey is a Connecticut landscape painter and member of the Guilford Art League. She is a keen observer of nature, and uses watercolor and gouache to study light on water "au plein aire." Joan is a founding member of the Shoreline ArtsTrail Open Studios event held each November in Branford, Guilford, and Madison, Connecticut.

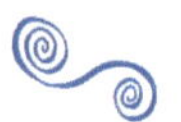

Joan is the founding director of a public (CREC*) and private collaborative, Center for Creative Youth. CCY is a national model pre-collage program for developing artistically talented youth at Wesleyan in Middletown, Connecticut. She had responsibility for the artistic, educational, and financial aspects for public and independent high school students in residence at CCY from 1976-1996. Today, more than 4,000 talented individuals attribute their professional careers in the arts and other fields to CCY. The Center for Creative Youth is celebrating its 40th anniversary in 2016.

Joan studied Spanish and Art at the University of Massachusetts (1963), the University of New Mexico, and in Mexico City. She taught with the International Schools Services in Colombia, South America and in Milan, Italy. She received her M.A. From Fairfield University, with Administration Certification from the University of Bridgeport and an M.A.L.S. from Wesleyan University in 1996.

Her collage series of icons, "Strong Courageous Women," began as an interdisciplinary thesis in Art History in 1994. Since then, selected pieces of the series have been exhibited at Zilka Gallery, Wesleyan University; Unitarian Society of New Haven; Hartford College for Women; Prague Conservatory, Czech Republic; the Guilford Free Library, and the Guilford Art Center.

The entire collection was featured in the exhibit *MYTH REDRAWN: Strong, Courageous Women*, hosted by the Mary C. Daly, RSM, Art Gallery at Mercy By the Sea in Madison, Connecticut from September to November, 2015.

Capitol Region Education Council, Connecticut

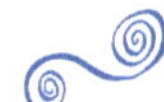

INTRODUCTION

***What can we learn from strong, courageous
women through the centuries?***

As a young girl, I observed that women demonstrate daily, courage, collaboration and creativity. Most women value relationships more than hierarchical position and power. Often, women's contributions go undocumented or uncelebrated. Throughout history there have been major discrepancies between a woman's life, honestly documented by her, and the current vogue of cultural attitudes. These mores and expectations, set by those dependent on her role, often dictate what is said, written or created about the female experience. Years of focused

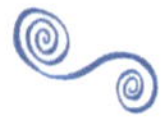

reading, study of the collective experience of woman from early times and travel to many cultures around the world have reduced the isolation of personal experience for me. I have frequently challenged the dominant view that women's heroic contributions to our lives and culture are subordinate to those of men. When the attributes of woman are reported through the lens of a journalist, historian or visual artist; who needs to preserve the traditional myths of male superiority, I have observed that the truth is colored, altered or diminished.

This series (1993-2015) of mixed media collages explores my deepest concerns in visual vocabulary. "Intruder objects" like collected images, my spontaneous watercolors, photographs, clippings and articles inspire me and document the anonymous work of woman as I continue to develop this symbolic vocabulary. I have for 22 years focused my study on representative artwork, iconography and selected readings from five historical periods: Prehistory, Antiquity, Medieval, Renaissance and Modern. My mixed media works depict my personal, emotional and intellectual reactions to the practice of diminishing women's contributions. My work attempts to symbolically elevate these contributions to the level of icons or prayer figures. Icons are concrete manifestations of the human and the spiritual.

From one woman's point of view, during this lifelong exploration, the icon becomes for me, a prayer, meditation, a reflective image. The multi-layering technique of collage is the merging of unrelated materials into a unified a whole. Collage lends itself to painterly layering of materials which reflects the multilayers of female experience. Using my handmade papers, I have committed to organizing fragments of women's history, contemporary readings, poetry and selected symbols to build a cohesive whole and to revise the myths.

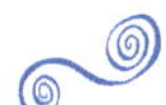

My icons seek to celebrate the sacred in the daily lives of women and depict the strength, courage, intuition and collaboration I observe in women's lives. My research has enabled me to rethink and study the spirituality of the early goddess and trace her influence and assimilation by religions of modern times. Elements of handmade lace and the spiral 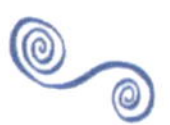 repeated in each work symbolize the anonymous work of women.

I have made an extensive study of the visual work of Judy Chicago, Romare Beardon, Joseph Cornell, Audrey Flack, Hannah Hock, Gino Severini, Kurt Switters, Miriam Shapiro and Nancy Spiro. I then studied the written work of the contemporary feminist art scholars Whitney Chadwick, Brandon Dijkstra, Elsa Honing Fine, Linda Nochlin and Ann Sutherland Harris.

I take my strongest advice from Bernard Chaet, Yale Art Professor Emeritus:

> *"There are no experts to show you the way. You have to experiment, and play with the materials,"*

I have experienced all the learning which takes place when one totally commits to solving an artistic problem which engages your intellect, your craft, and your emotions. This series, an intensive labor, has continued over time to give me enormous personal pleasure. Somewhere during the experience, I released the burden of anger, which I have carried since childhood. These familiar scars can be seen in the lack of confidence in young girls and women who grow up in a collective culture which does not preserve and nurture emotional, social, educational and financial equality for females. Our individual opportunities and success are in direct proportion to our strength to rebel.

In this collection of works, I have tried to challenge the politics of the representation of women. We have the golden nugget of reproduction; why not choose the golden nugget of courage, energy, strength, power and financial independence?

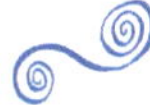

THE ICONS

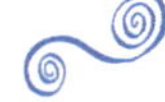

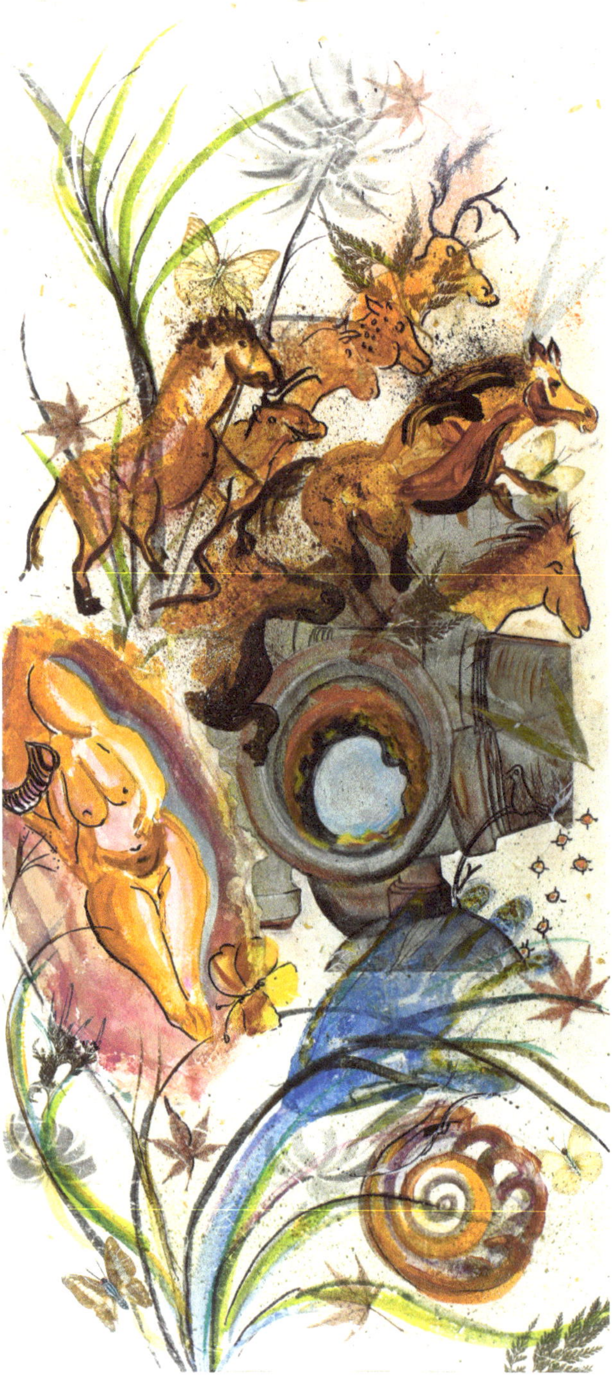

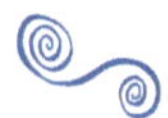

Rock Stars

(30,000 B.C.E., 16"w x 24"h)

The *Rock Stars* icon recreates Stone Age cavewomen's paintings found in the caves of Lauscaux, France and dated 30,000 B.C.E. This icon is a celebration of the life-giving force of women, depicting pregnant mares, children's handprints, and symbols of the feminine. Archaeologists have discovered mitochondria DNA, found only in women, in the saliva mix that was used in blowpipes. Pigments of crushed sepia, yellow ochre, burnt sienna and charcoal were blown onto the rocks. The signature is of women, men and children artists working together. These murals that depict excitement and movement are still brilliant today. The Virgin of Laussel, with her horn with 13 marks, is in a cave nearby. The murals suggest that collaboration is the gateway to survival and life.

Note: Mitochondrial Eve is "the most recent woman from whom all living humans today descend, in an unbroken line, on their mother's side, and through the mothers of those mothers, and so on, back until all lines converge on one person." Her presence is an important reminder that there is very little difference between all of us.

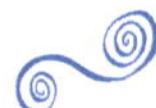

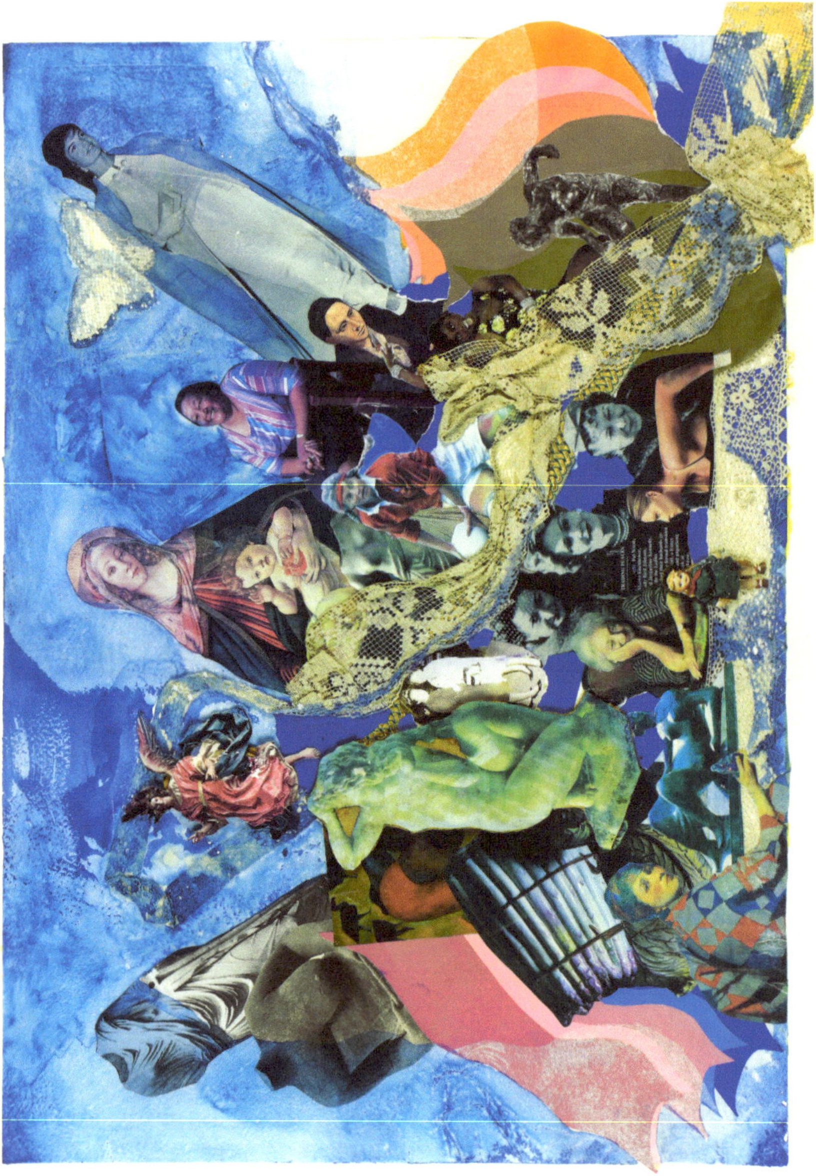

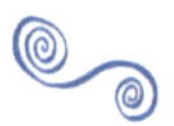

SKY ALTAR TO OPTIMA PRINCIPESA: THE GREAT MOTHER

(Antiquity 2,500 B.C.E., 34-3/4"w x 24-3/4"h)

The *Sky Altar to Optima Principesa: The Great Mother* honors all mothers: Isis, Aphrodite; our great grandmothers and grandmothers; our own mothers. Images of mothers throughout the centuries beg the viewer to consider: what were their challenges? Here, lace has become a symbol of the invisible work of women. This symbol is carried throughout the collection of icons.

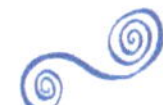

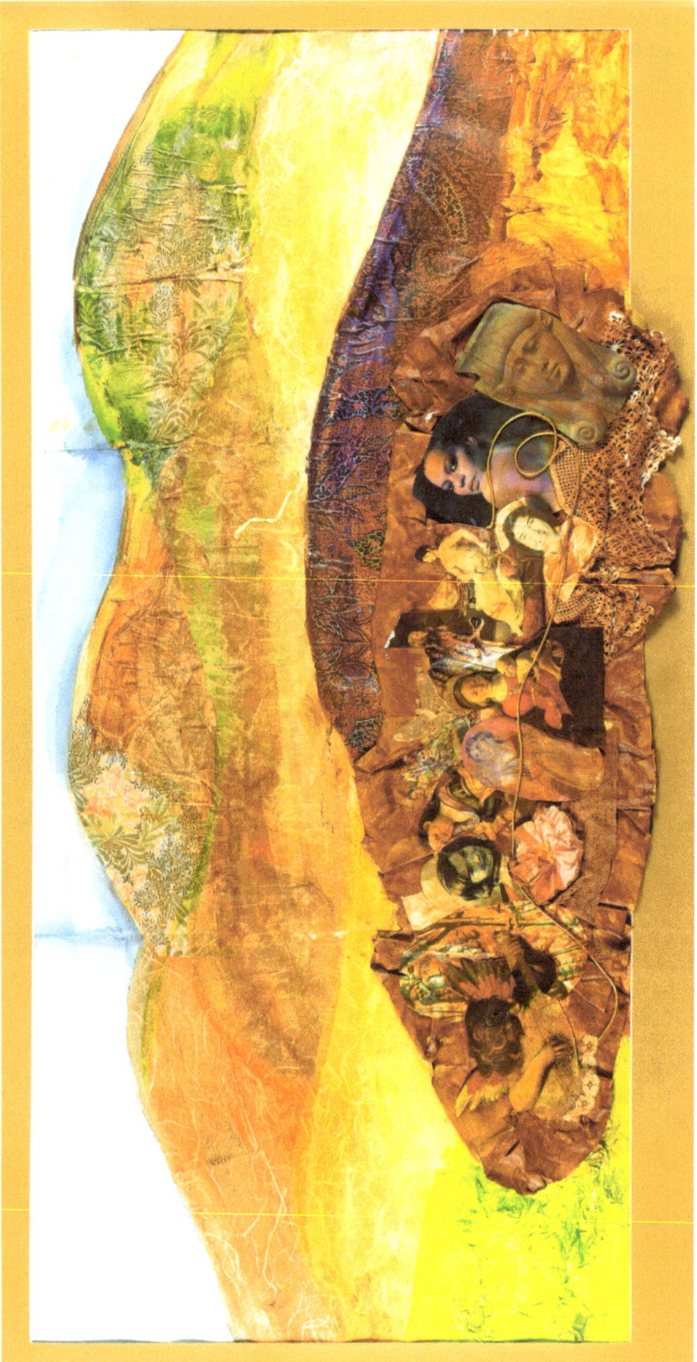

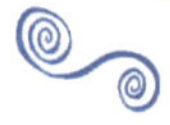

3 THE GREAT GODDESS: REGENERATRIX OF THERA

(Antiquity 2,500 B.C.E., 46"w x 24-3/4"h)

Feminine, curving shapes in *The Great Goddess: Regeneratrix of Thera* represent the sacred places on earth. The curves of the earth, through the centuries, have welcomed builders to make spiritual centers, sacred places, for the continuity of life. Think of the Grand Canyon, the pyramids of Egypt, Tenochtitlan, Mexico, the Acropolis, Greece Chartres, France, or the caves of Meath, Ireland. The fish is an ancient symbol of faith. These spiritual centers affirm the continuity of life in the same way we find affirmation in the faces of our sacred mothers.

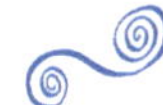

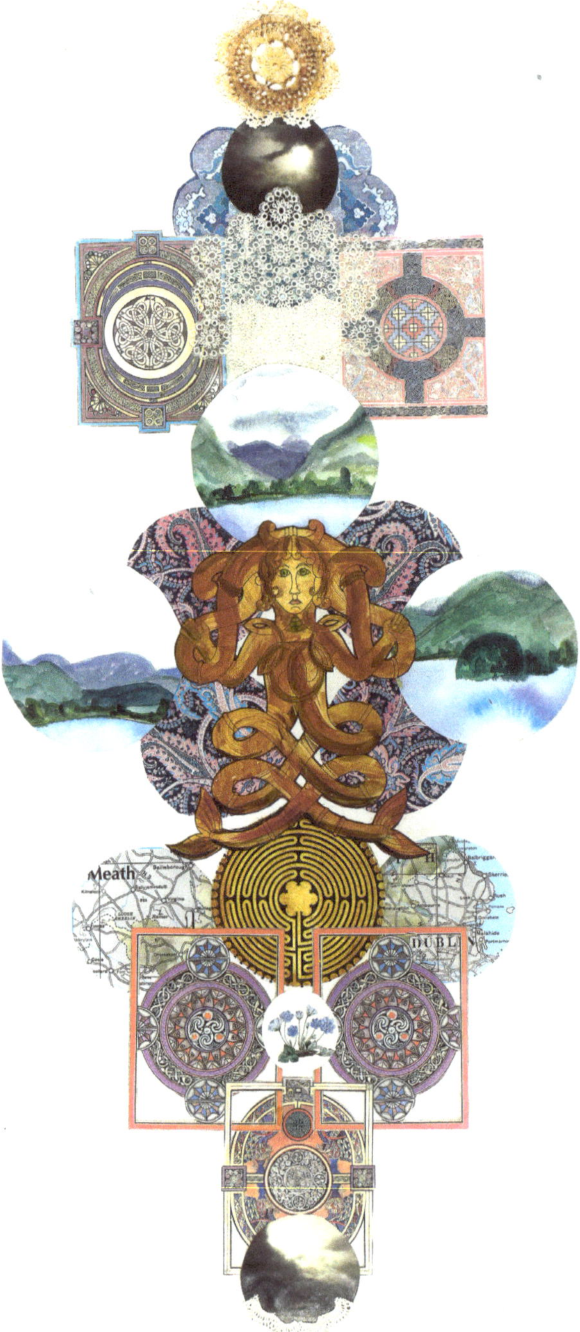

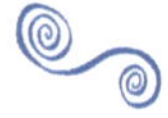

4 Bridget's Cross: Mother of Healing and Fire

(453 - 1329 A.D., 16"w x 24"h)

Bridget's Cross icon honors Bregheta, or Saint Brigit of Kildare (450-525 AD), an Irish nun and champion of the poor. She was the abbess of an immense double monastery one side for women, the other for men. Her feast day, February 1, celebrates the hope of spring, and coincides with the festival of Imbolc honoring the pre-Christian goddess Brigid. Corn dolls are made in her honor today in Ireland. Within this icon, images ask us to think about how in Bridget's day a woman might inherit land, but upon her death, it passed to male, not female, relatives. Today you can visit her, the patron saint of artists, farmers, and teachers—St. Bridget stands at the left of the main door in St. Patrick's Cathedral in New York City. Lace from Ireland is the "intruder object" in this work. An intruder object in collage making is the spark that urges the artist to make the piece.

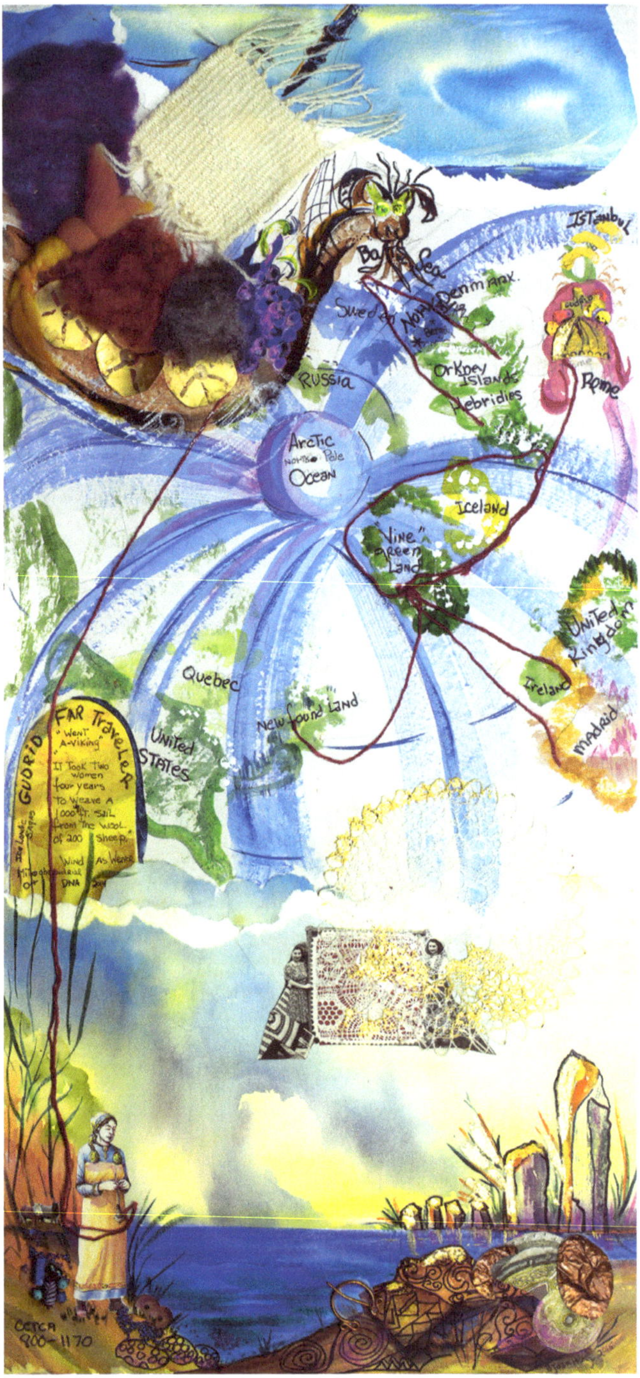

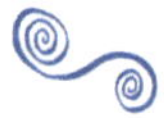

Istanbul
Baltic Sea
Sweden
Norway
Denmark
Russia
Orkney Islands
Hebridies
Rome
Arctic Ocean
North Pole
Iceland
"Vine" Green Land
United Kingdom
Ireland
Madrid
Quebec
United States
New Found Land
GUDRID FAR TRAVELER
"Went A-Viking"
It took two women four years to weave a 1,000 sq ft sail from the wool of 200 sheep.
Woven through mitochondrial DNA
As woven
Circa 900-1170

Women Went "a Viking"
(1030 - 1066 A.D., 16"w x 24"h)

Like the threads in a woven cloth, the contributions of women are vast and varied. In the early eleventh century, it would take two women four years to weave a 1,000 sq. ft. sail from the wool of 200 of their sheep for the swift Viking ships. The large square rigged sail of red and natural grey made an impressive sight on the seas. DNA evidence from graves has shown women dyed with cochineal red dye from South America and royal purple from local lichen. Women's craft was immensely valued from 1030 to 1066. "Wind as Weaver."

According to the Norse Tales, Gudrid, the far traveler made a pilgrimage to Vinland and as far as Rome and Istanbul. Archaeologists used carbon dating and DNA analysis to examine her grave. Extensive treasures were found. Colorful textiles along with mitochondrial DNA proved women were travelers. Archaeologists found rich copper & gold broaches, silver, amber, cobalt beads, and Celtic spiral designs. They also found evidence of wine making, vineyards and harvest. Vinland could be Iceland, or Newfoundland. Viking women led settlements during the absence of men.

Viking women's red and royal purple textiles were a status symbol and a major commodity for trade. As valuable as plundering; textiles were the Viking's "cash crop."

Today in Scotland, if you go for tea, scones or a wee bit of scotch, you will find intricate Shetland and Orkney lace patterns informed by elegant Celtic designs.

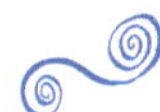

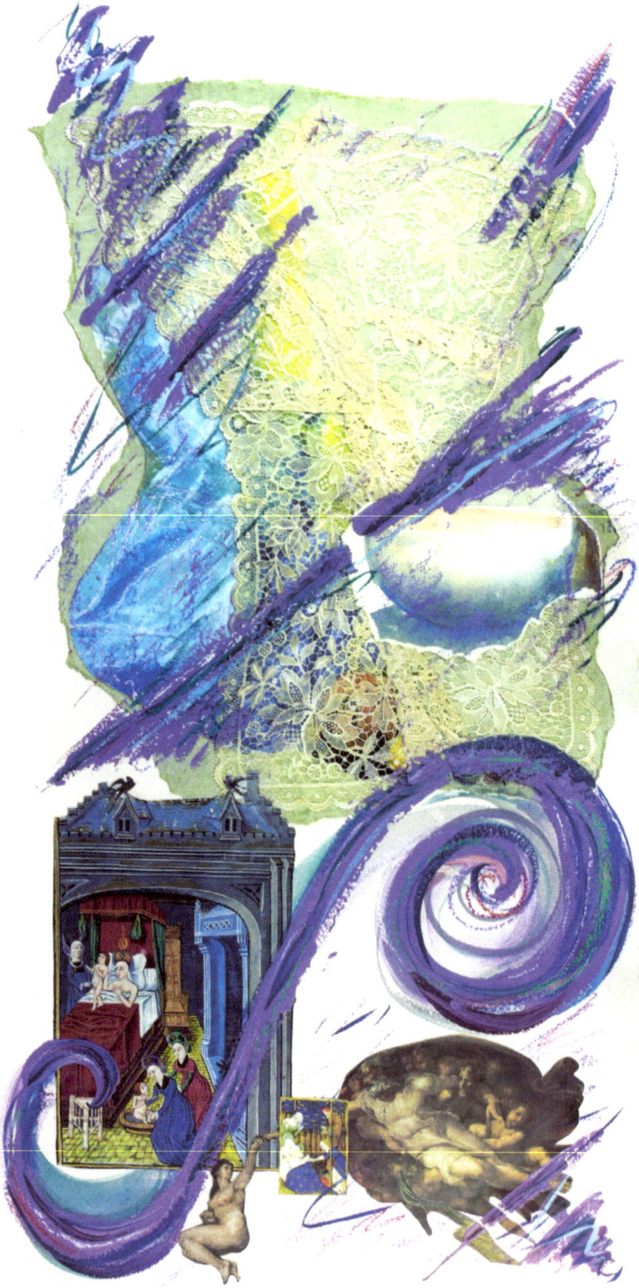

BIRTH SHRINE TO EVE
(Circa 80 B.C.E. - 1550 A.D., 16"w x 24"h)

For centuries, women have helped women in all civilizations give birth in caves, tents, temples, huts, stables, cottages and mansions. The icon, *Birth Shrine to Eve* celebrates women with symbols of the feminine; birth and the divine mother Eve. The Sistine Chapel by Michelangelo informs this icon imagining the God that gives women the gift and power to make life… redrawing the myth. Elements of handmade lace from Rome and a spiral design symbolize the anonymous and ongoing work of women.

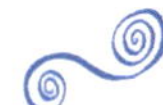

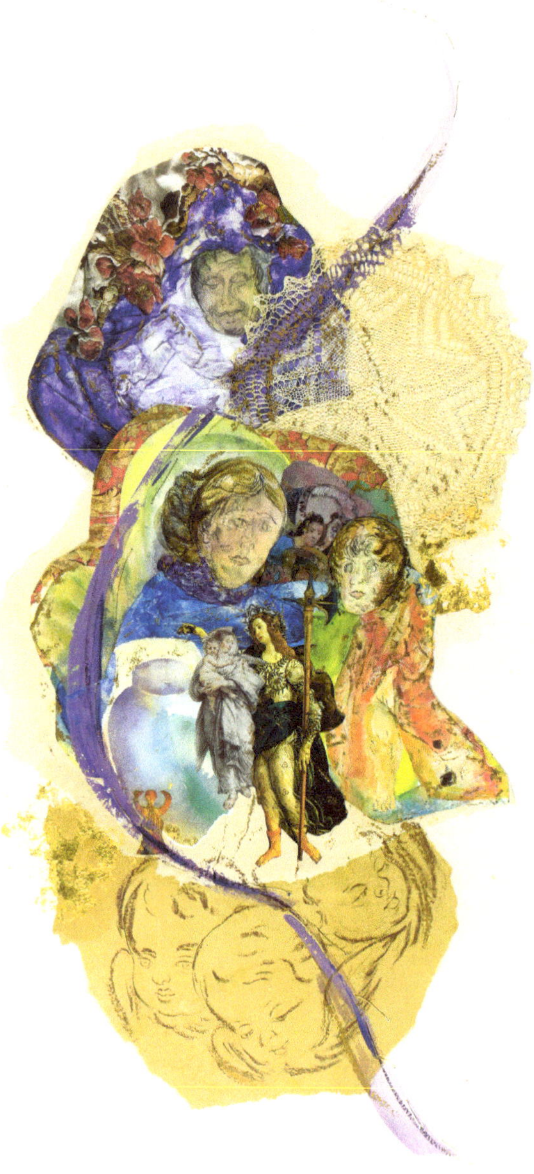

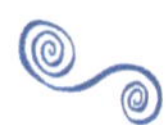

MADONNA, MOTHER, WARRIOR QUEEN
(Renaissance 1450 - 1550 A.D., 16"w x 24"h)

Madonna, Mother, Warrior Queen depicts the many faces and roles of women, as sacred symbols, as mothers and grandmothers, as leaders and warriors. Lace and gold threads from Florence, Italy are a symbol and metaphor for grandmothers sewing the generations together. This multifaceted role is present through the ages, in Greek and Roman art, during the Renaissance, and in modern times.

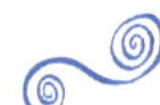

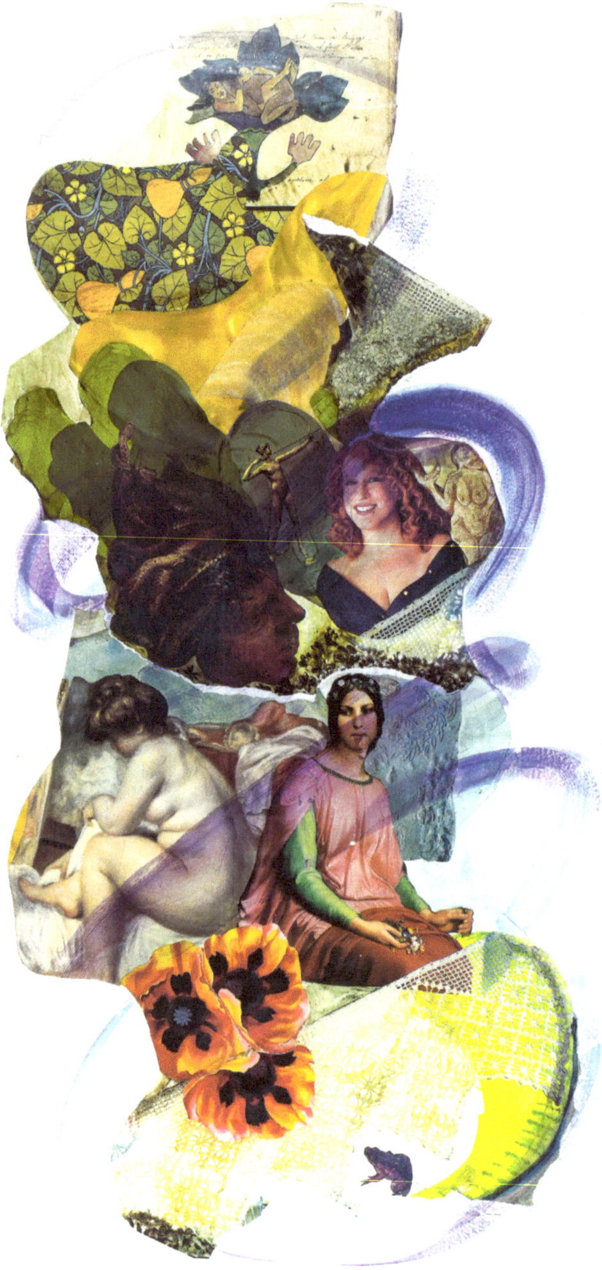

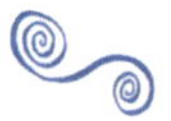

MEDUSA'S POWER

(Renaissance 1450 - 1550 A.D., 16"w x 24"h)

Beautiful women come in many sizes and shapes. Images of Rubenesque women have been chosen for this icon in praise of the feminine body. The bronze goddess Diana, the huntress, with her bow and arrow demonstrate strength and action. Sappho comes from the Latin for frog. Here she represents ancient wisdom from Sappho, the Greek woman poet. Medusa's head with all her snakes and curls cautions all women to listen to their intuition and express healthy anger when necessary to protect themselves.

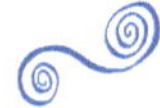

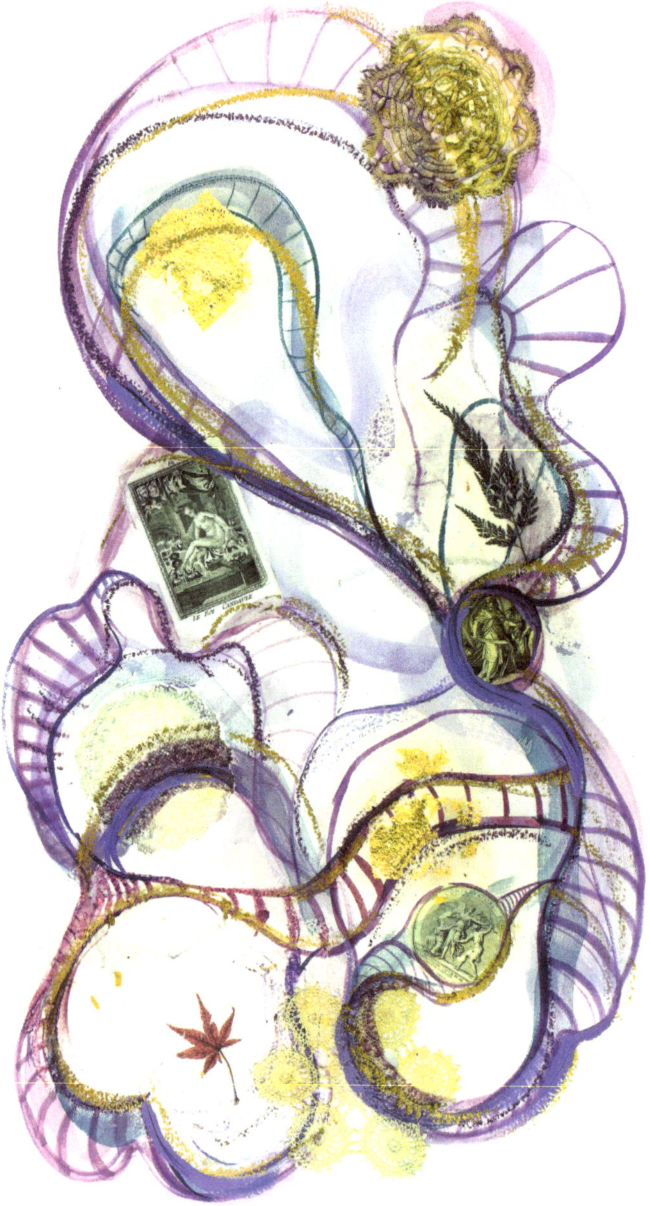

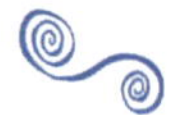

STRENGTH, WISDOM AND COURAGE
(450 B.C.E. - 1660 A.D., 16"w x 24"h)

Warrior woman defend yourself! In the deuterocanonical
Book of Judith, the Jewish heroine Judith cuts off the head of
Holofernes, an invading military general and saves her people.
It is a favorite subject in Medieval, Renaissance, Baroque art
and literature that illustrates the archetypal power of women.
Artemisia Gentileschi, Baroque painter, was inspired in 1620 to
create her masterpiece with this theme. The *Strength, Wisdom
and Courage* icon depicts Judith, her soft, lush womanly
body contrasting with the determined spirit in defense of her
homeland, her family, and her power to create life.

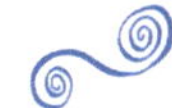

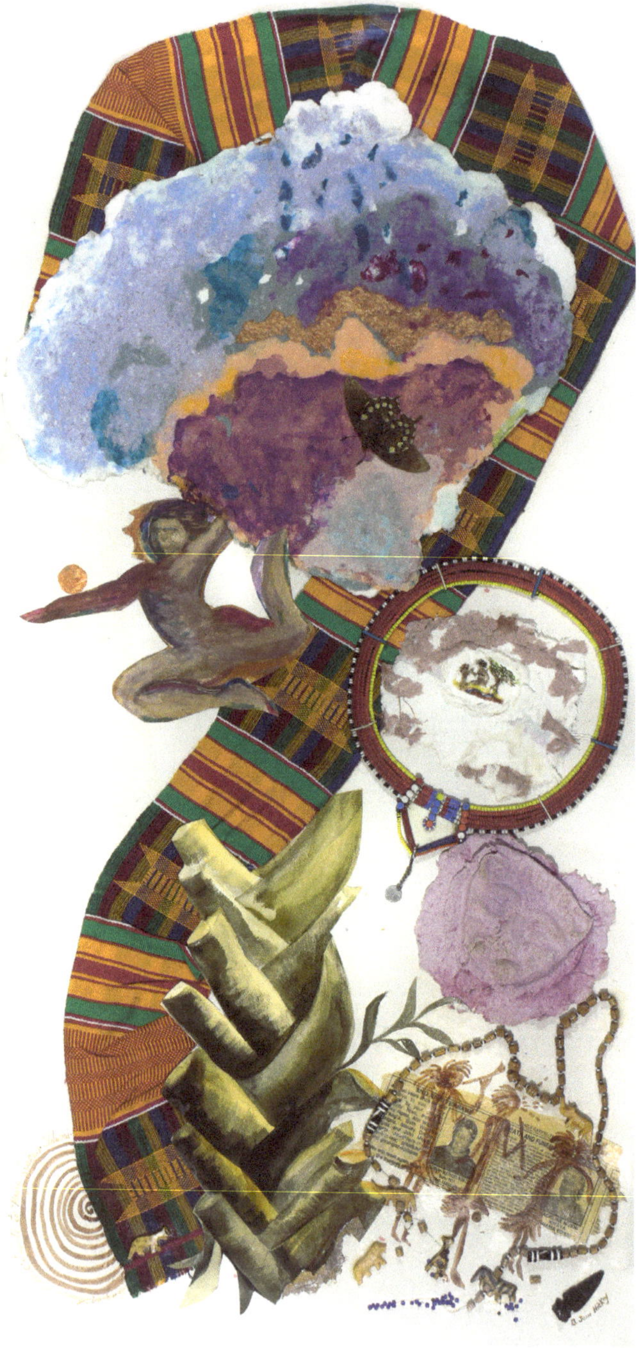

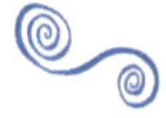

10 Black Madonna Brings Spiritual Courage

(1200 - 2000 A.D., 16"w x 24"h)

The Black Madonna icon shows Artemis the huntress, representing the spiritual courage of the mother lionesses from Africa. The repeated images of woven textiles and spirals, here an authentic Kente cloth and beadwork, reiterate the anonymous and ongoing work of women. Jennifer Davies, fiber artist, gave me her handmade papers, the intruder objects that sparked the beginnings of this work. The work was inspired by a trip to Africa in 2008.

In 2015, this collage was dedicated to Misty Copeland, as she became the first African American woman to be named a principal in the 75-year history of The American Ballet Theater. Her memoir *Life in Motion: An Unlikely Ballerina* and her illustrated children's book *Firebird*, tell her story to multiple generations. One of Misty's finest hours was dancing *The Firebird* choreographed by George Balanchine.

Upon giving this collage a careful reading, an eight-year-old girl, Katy said, "When Misty was told she couldn't be a classical ballerina, she felt cut down like the stump of the African tree." Her friend Riley J. responded, "Moths can survive the heat, Misty flies like a moth or butterfly."

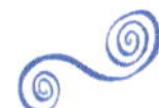

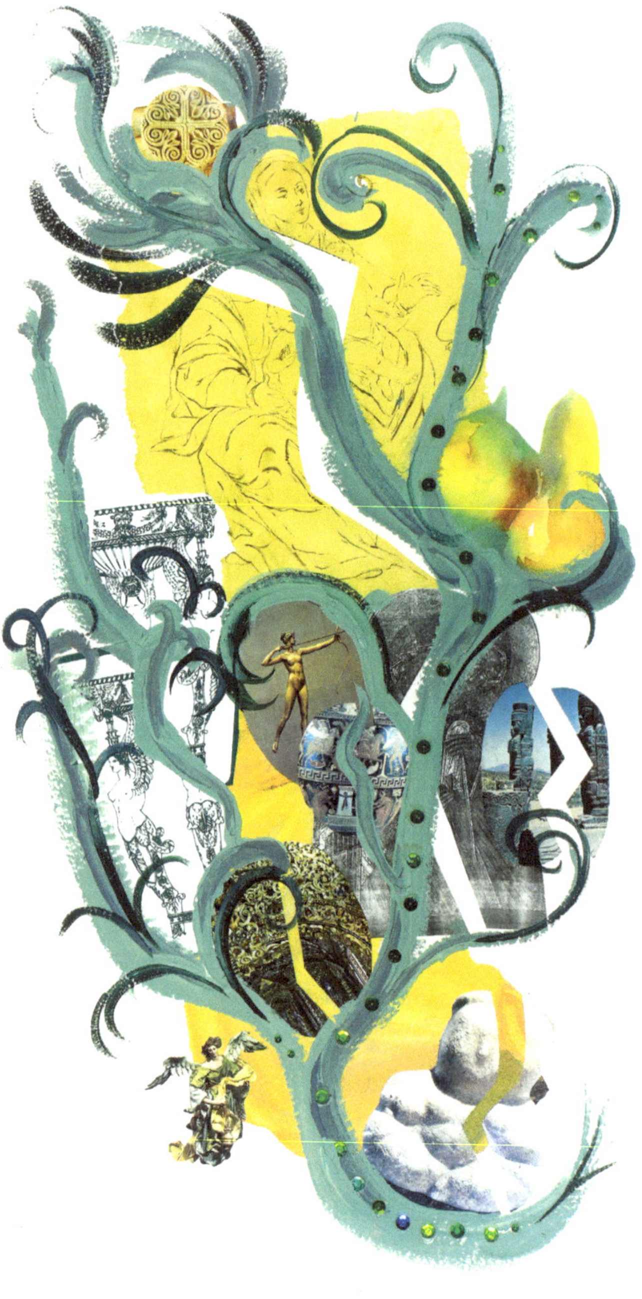

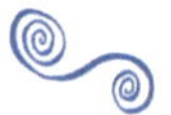

11 THE TREE OF LIFE
(1700 - 1850 A.D., 16"w x 24"h)

The Tree of Life reminds us that we are all part of the greater cycle, sustained by and sustaining the earth. Etchings found in an antique shop were the starting point for this piece. Diana the huntress, a constellation, and sculptures in marble and bronze, have inspired Greeks, Romans and modern day viewers worldwide to aim high. In this icon, new shoots are represented by the spiral element to move towards a future of peace, harmony and justice for all.

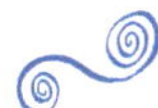

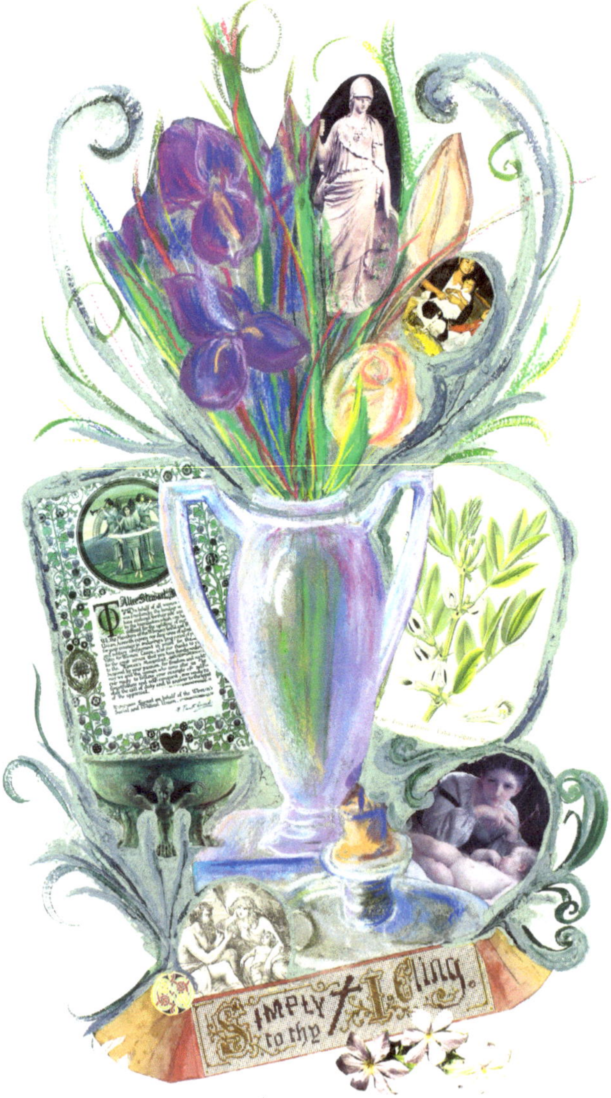

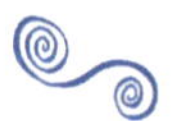

Simply to thy † Cling.
to thy

12 Athena: Fève Vulgaire

(1700 - 1850 A.D., 16"w x 24"h)

The ugly seed packet was the catalyst /"intruder object" for this icon. "Vanitas" is a romantic form of still life painting used in this collage. This work is a celebration of the vagina, precious to women; ridiculed by some voices in the misogynist sectors of our culture. The early 20th century artist Georgia O'Keefe celebrated the vagina in her varied collection of flower paintings, in my view. An elegant vase of flowers in original watercolors combined with an image of the Greek goddess Athena's strength, lend the symbolism to this icon.

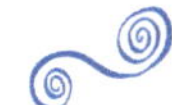

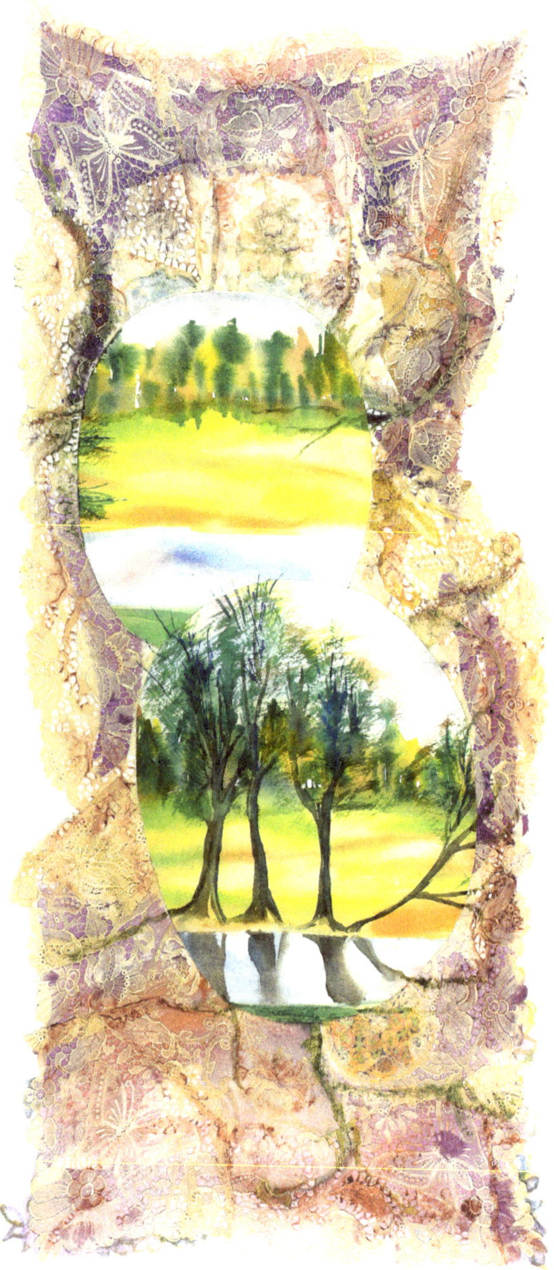

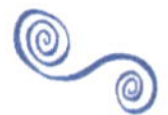

INTUITION

(16"w x 24"h)

Intuition reflects upon what is often called "the woman's gift," the ability to understand something immediately without the need for linear, conscious reasoning. All research leads to the plastic nature of the male and female brain. Unfortunately, our total potential development is dependent on social norms, collective culture, economic and health opportunities. In this collage, intuition is celebrated with authentic Belgian lacework and original watercolors to invoke the quiet and the concentration required to receive the gift of intuition.

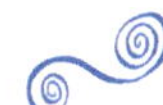

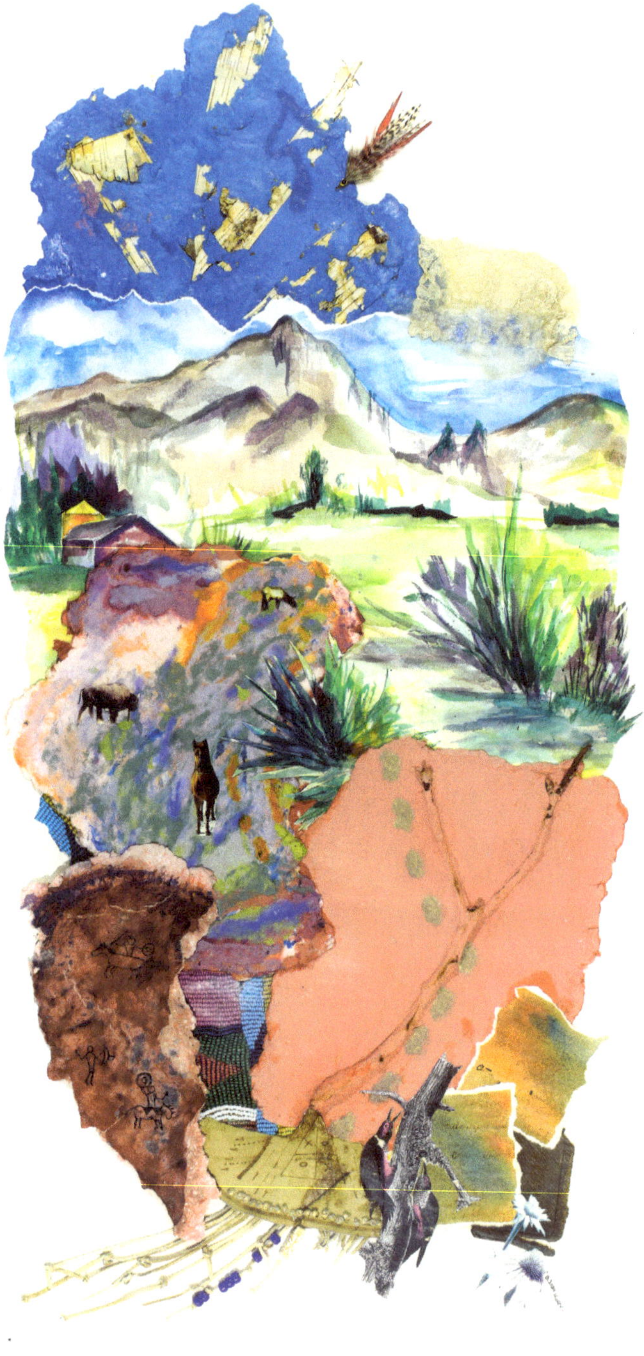

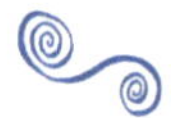

 # SACAGAWEA
(1700 - 1850 A.D., 16"w x 24"h)

Sacagawea narrates the story of the Shoshone guide on the Lewis & Clark expedition in the early 1800s. She is said to have carried her infant son on her back for much of the journey, more than 4,000 miles. She could speak the native languages. She swam to save equipment; she could identify flora and fauna and natural medicine for naturalist Meriwether Lewis; and she knew the way. The main symbol is the forked stick, a found object. As a direct result of her efforts, the Corps of Discovery of the Louisiana Territory doubled the size of the United States of America, but Sacagawea was not rewarded with land from President Thomas Jefferson, as were the others of the Corps of Discovery. William Clark had great respect for Sacagawea and had conflict with her trapper husband Charbineau over her cruel treatment. At one point she replaced every man's moccasins. Her cobalt beads were traded for the horses the explorers rode to reach the Pacific. It took close to 200 years for her contributions to be recognized by the United States, most notably with a U.S. dollar coin commemorating her leadership.

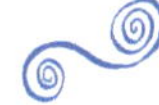

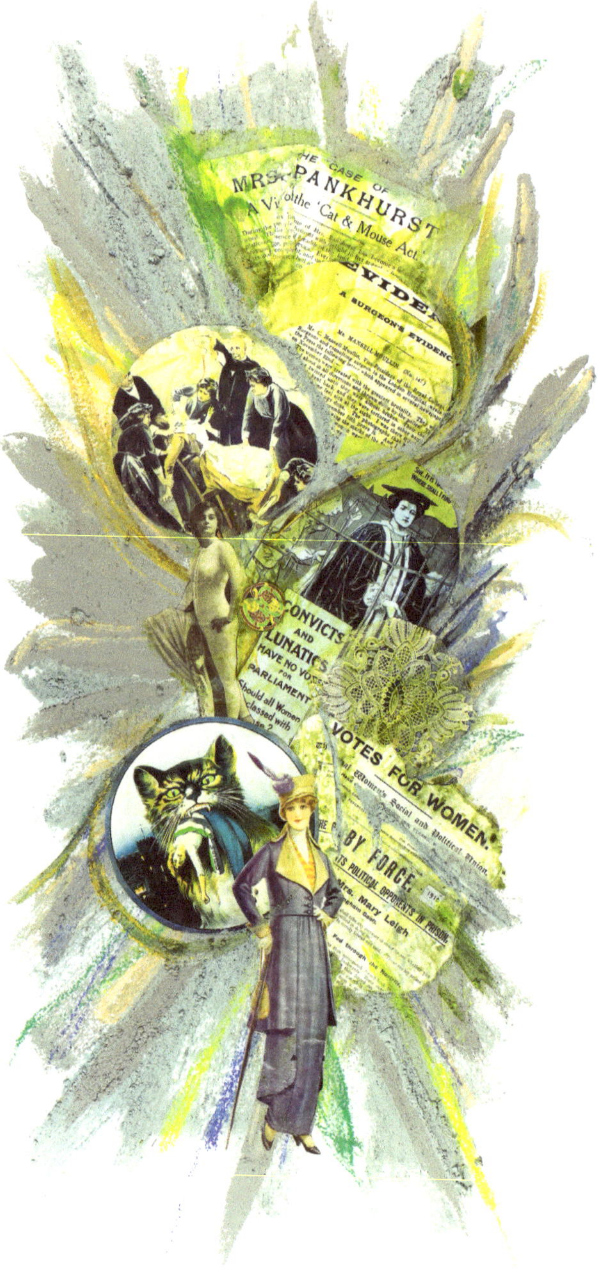

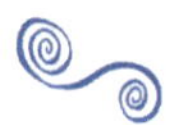

CAT AND MOUSE: VOTES FOR WOMEN!!!
(1900 - 1960 A.D., 16"w x 24"h)

Cat & Mouse represents the struggle of women to gain the right to vote. The catalyst for this icon was a copy of a real newspaper story from the London Museum. British suffragettes [Mrs. Elizabeth Pankhurst] were force fed during jailing in a hunger strike. British and American newspaper headlines from as early as 1910 narrated the fight, but victory came slowly. American suffragettes learned from their British sisters. In the U.S., Montana was the first state to give women the right to vote…in 1920.

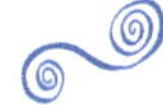

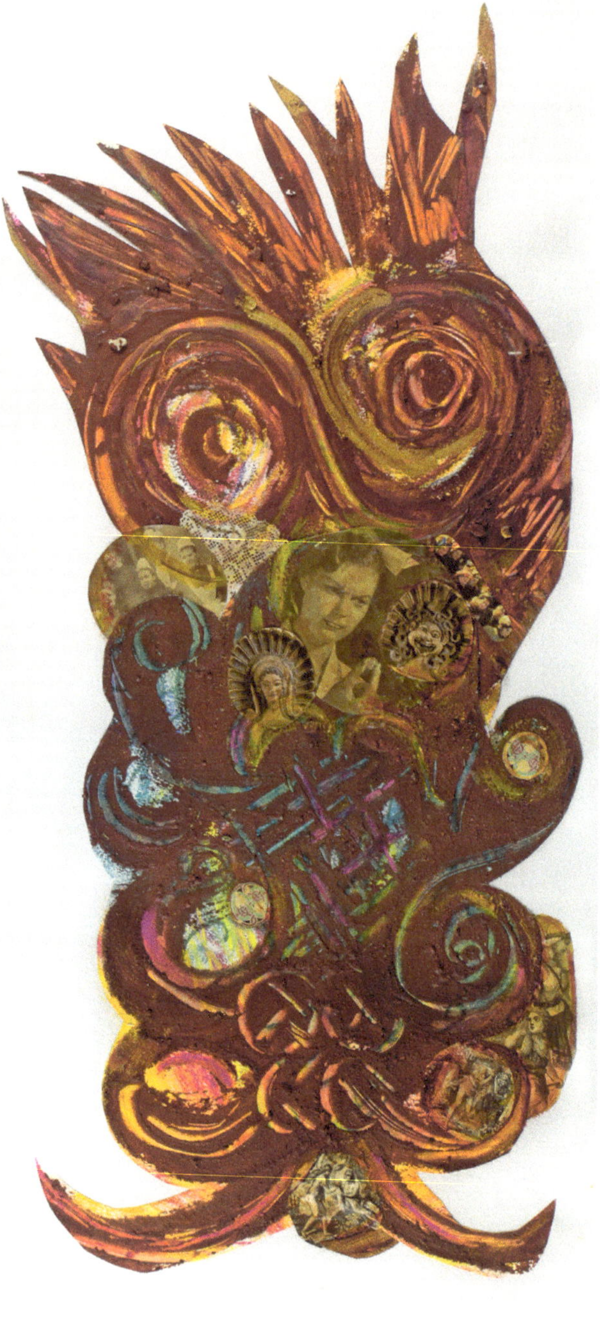

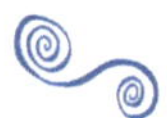

ANOTHER NICKEL TIP

(1900 - 1960 A.D., 16"w x 24"h)

The colors in this collage depict an explosion of fire and anger. Women have to be very skilled not to have their contributions devalued. For example, "Do you work?" in this culture means outside the home. As if managing a home and a family of children or elders were not work. The sub-text is that only paid work is valued. Women who work outside the home, full-time, still spend three times the amount of time on household chores then men. Lace caps, aprons, the nurses, this waitress's face, the expressive Etruscan sculptured faces [750 B.C.E. to 250 B.C.E.] demonstrate the anger women have felt since Eve was blamed for the "apple" incident. Celtic knots, fiery emotions and the spiral and the lace are elements that are repeated in all 25 collages. The article from 1950 echoes Peggy Lee's own composition "Is that all there is?" It is a familiar question posed by women in an unfair work situation or one-sided relationship.

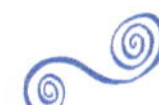

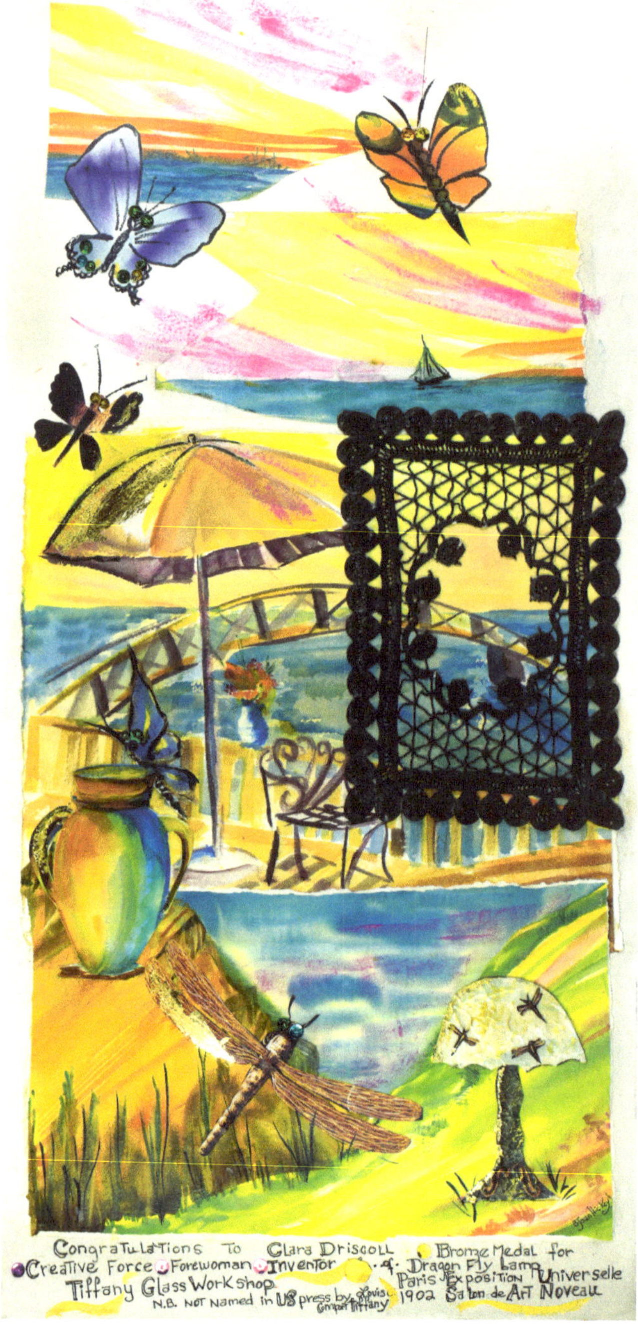

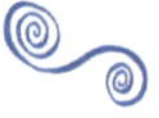

Congratulations To Clara Driscoll   Bronze Medal for
Creative Force Forewoman Inventor   4. Dragon Fly Lamp
Tiffany Glass Workshop   Paris Exposition Universelle
N.B. Not Named in US press by Louis C. Comfort Tiffany 1902 Salon de Art Noveau

17 WOMAN INVENTS TIFFANY LAMP

(1900 - 1960 A.D., 16"w x 24"h)

Aesthetic Movement, 1890-1905. The Tiffany lamp invented and designed by Clara Driscoll won first prize at the prestigious Paris Exhibition of Art Noveau in 1902. Her dragonfly lamp won the bronze medal. Her achievement was never publicized by Tiffany & Company in this country. Tiffany went on to sell hundreds of lamps with her original floral designs of poppies, peacocks, wisteria and more. From her boarding house in New York City, Clara rode her bike to gardens in Yonkers to make original watercolors. Clara oversaw the Tiffany workshop from 1892-1908, but her contributions would not be known for another 100 years. Her work was featured in the book *Clara and Mr. Tiffany* by Susan Vreeland, and in the 2006 New York Historical Society's exhibit titled "A New Light on Tiffany."

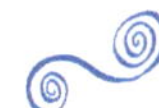

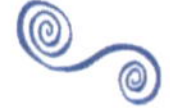

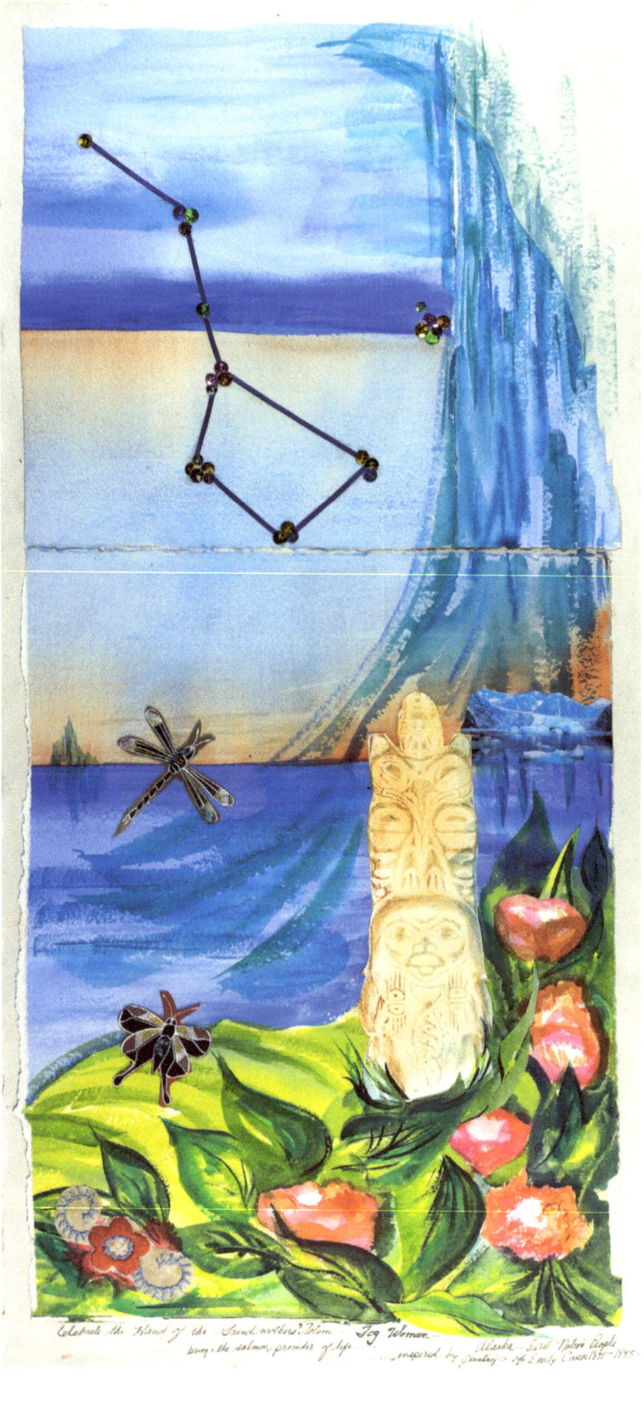

Celebrate the Hand of the Grandmothers' Totem ... Fog Woman...
bring the salmon provider of life
Alaska ... First Nation People
inspired by paintings of Emily Carr 1871 - 1945.

ALASKA: TOTEM TO GRANDMOTHER FOG WHO BRINGS IN THE SALMON

(1900 - 1960 A.D., 16"w x 24"h)

Early Alaskan artist Emily Carr (1871-1945) said "Art is art… nature is nature, you cannot improve upon it." Her work was inspired in part by the indigenous "first nation" peoples of the Pacific Northwest Coast. So, too, is this collage, which depicts a rare totem pole with the likeness of Fog Woman. Also known as Grandmother Fog, she is the provider of salmon and life in early spring to first nation people. Familiar scenes in Alaska include the Big Dipper and the North Star, included here for their guiding presence. The original watercolors remind us of the importance of attending to the melting ice cap.

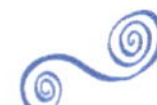

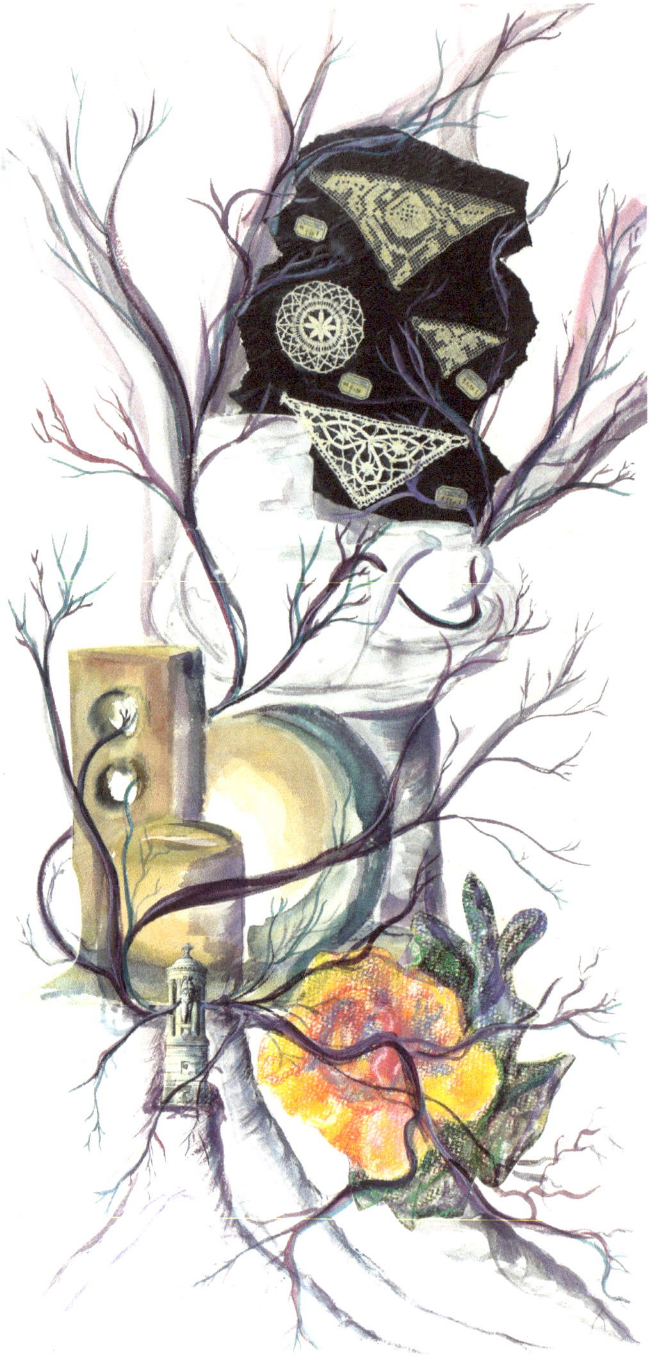

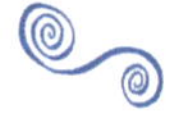

BAUBO: THE BELLY GODDESS /AUTONOMY

(Past into Future, 16"w x 24"h)

Baubo is an ancient sculpture from 400 B.C.E, the goddess of mirth. She celebrates the transformational affect of laughter and healing in black humor. Women friends connect with each other with belly laughs about their bodies and sensuality. It is the epitome of the sacred sexual, combining heat, passion, and a vivacious energy for life. *Baubo, The Belly Goddess* bids women to honor and respect their own bodies, growing older, with strength, courage and a touch of humor. The Belgian lace sampler was a lucky find in an antique shop in Antwerp, Belgium. This icon celebrates older women's passion and energy for life.

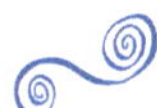

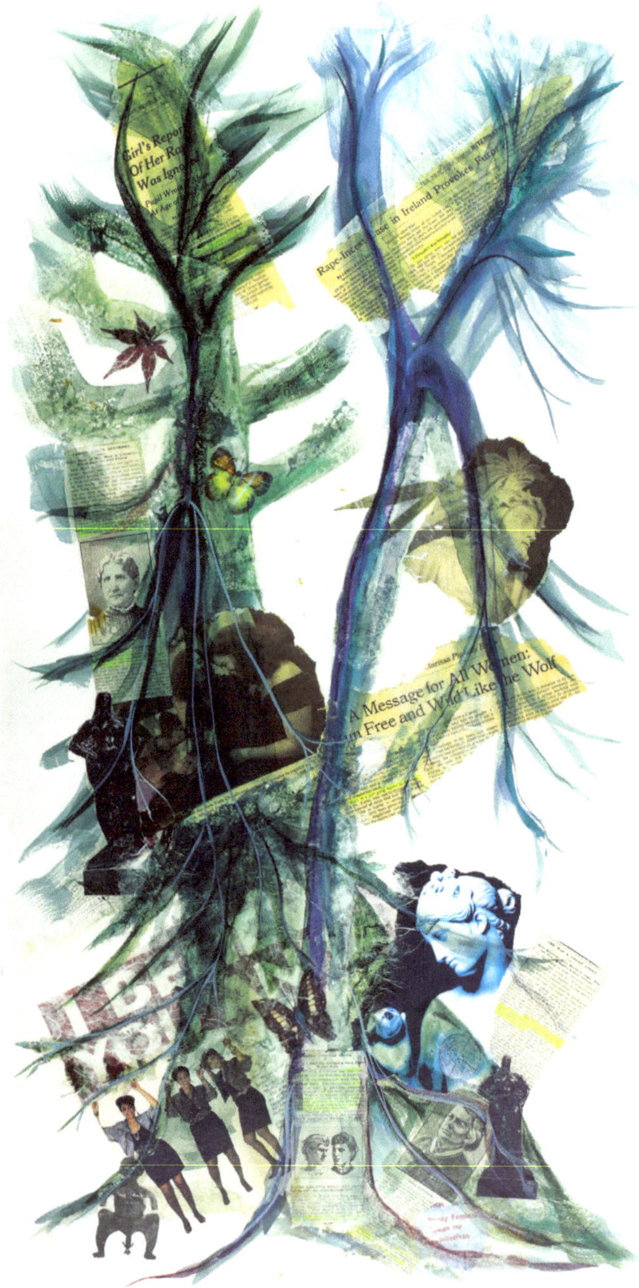

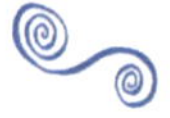

BRAVE CHICAGO GIRLS:
WE BELIEVE YOU ANITA HILL

(Past into Future, 16"w x 24"h)

Multiple images spanning more than a 100 years influence the
Brave Chicago Girls icon. Within this piece, the viewer learns
about: two brave nurses in the Spanish American War [1898],
who worked against yellow fever, 19th century master painter
of majestic animals Rosa Bonheur sketched in slaughter houses,
suffragist Mary Livermore, and sexual harassment trailblazer
Anita Hill. Keeping company with Eve, the piece invokes the
power and hard-won battles of women.

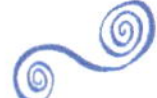

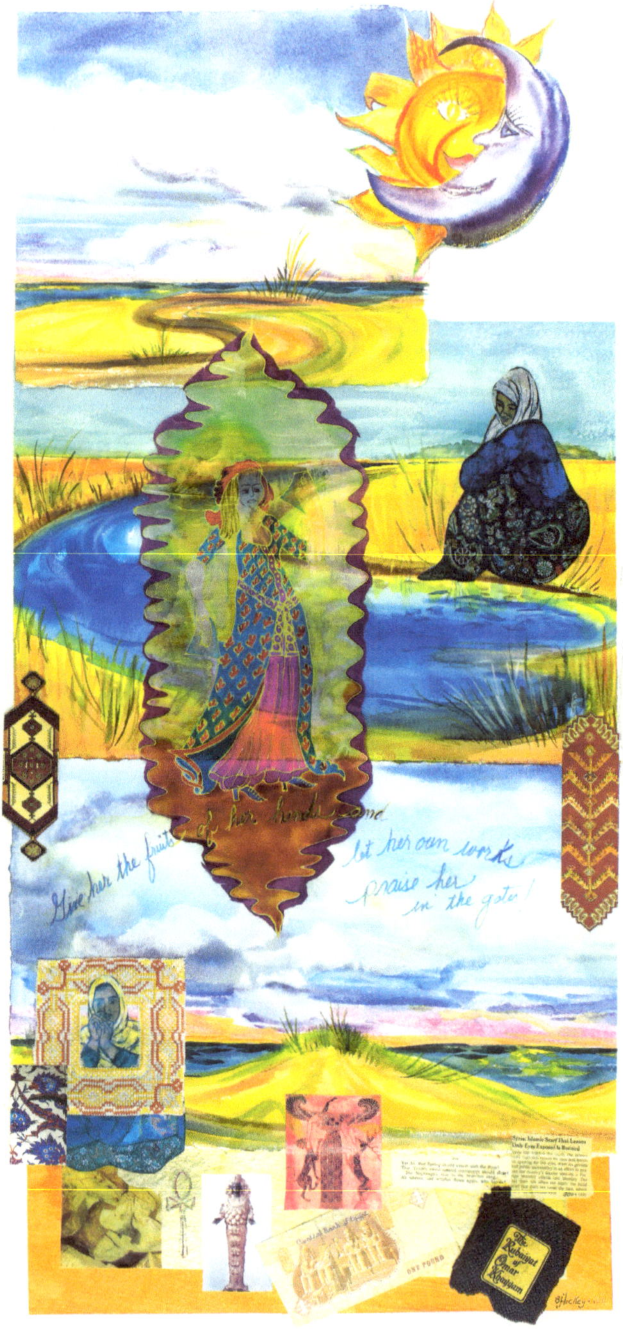

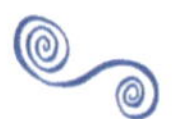

Give her the fruit of her hands and
let her own works
praise her
in the gates!

 # PATHWAYS TO COLLABORATION: MALALA

(Past into Future, 16"w x 24"h)

"Give her the fruits of her hands and let her own works praise her in the gates." This impassioned phrase from Proverbs sets the tone for the *Pathways to Collaboration: Malala* icon. The silk batik and the fragment of a poem by Omar Khayyam [1048-1120] are from a market in Istanbul. The icon is a harmonious blend of strong colors and bold patterns symbolizing the results of working together, the fruits of our collective labors. The watercolor elements were done near the Gulf of Aqaba in the Red Sea near the beautiful deserts and mountains of the Middle East. The burka, the abaya, the hijab; these required fashions are about control not a personal statement. The icon recognizes Malala Yousafzai, the 17-year-old Pakistani activist and the youngest Nobel Prize [2014] winner. Malala, a strong, young woman, boldly worked on behalf of all women to fight for the education of young girls in her country. "The girl who was shot for going to school."

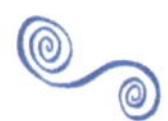

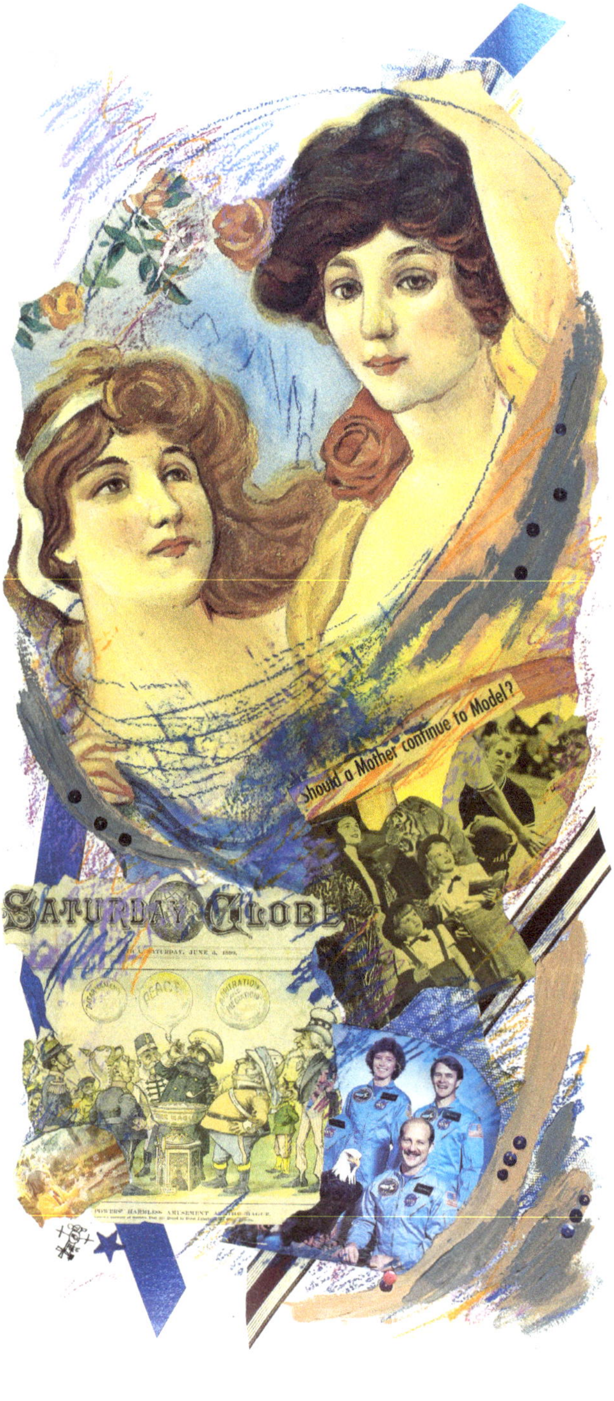

Should a Mother continue to Model?
SATURDAY GLOBE

22

SHOULD A MOTHER CONTINUE TO MODEL?

(1960 A.D. - Present, 16"w x 24"h)

Should a Mother Continue to Model? was inspired by a 1960s newspaper article. The fragment of an opera poster from Rome provides the elegance. As Russian leaders make bubbles for peace again; an autobiographical sketch, a tiny girl's art, is the beginning of a distinguished university career in the Arts. Using varied media this icon presents the juxtaposition of the perceived roles of women versus the notable achievements of women like Sally Ride, an American astrophysicist, and the first American woman in space. Sally Ride blasts through the glass ceiling!

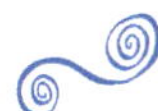

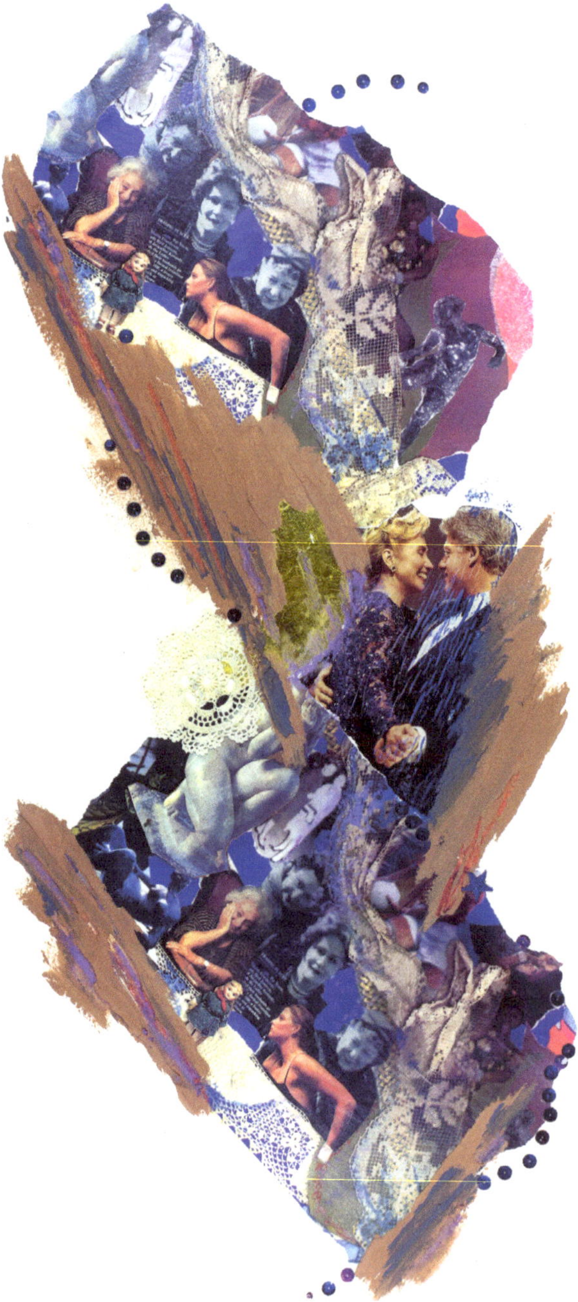

23

TRADING PLACES

(1960 A.D. - Present, 16"w x 24"h)

This icon made in 1996 has special significance today. *Trading Places* tells the story of many first ladies. Hillary Clinton is a brilliant feminist who has lived and worked all of her life for economic, political and social equality for women. Educated at Wellesley College and Yale University in the early 1970s, Hillary went on to work as an attorney advocating for children and families. She authored the book *It Takes a Village: and Other Lessons Children Teach Us* in 1996 while serving as First Lady with President Bill Clinton. She went on to become a New York State Senator, ran for President in 2008, and was appointed by President Barack Obama to serve as Secretary of State. In 2014, she became a grandmother, just nine months prior to announcing her second run for President of the United States in 2016. She is the only first lady to hold national office. She doesn't like baking cookies and that's OK.

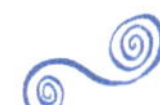

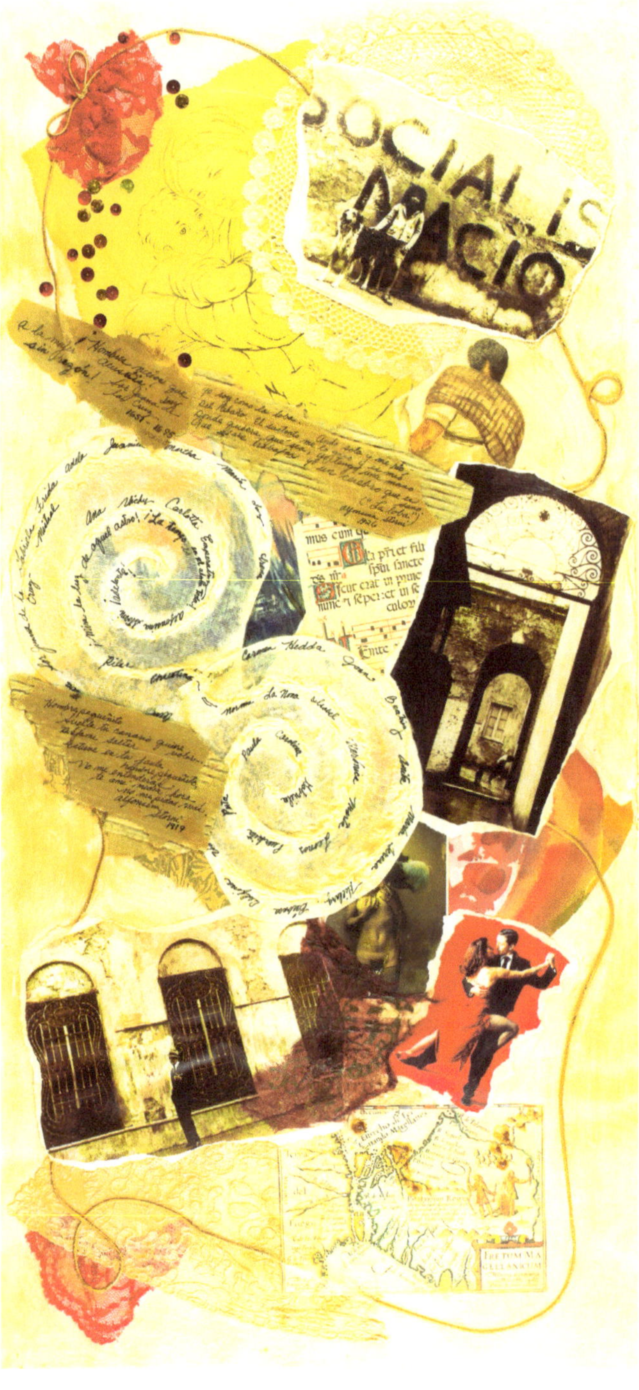

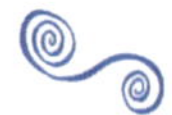

24 LA LOBA: PROTECT YOURSELF, BE LIKE THE FEMALE WOLF

(1960 A.D. - Present, 16"w x 24"h)

This icon is inspired by several trips to Latin America. *La Loba* is a tribute to strong female voices from Cuba, Argentina, Chile, Columbia, and Mexico who speak for the protection of women. It honors writers like Sor Juana de la Cruz (1650-1695), featured on the 200 Mexican peso, who wrote about "Hombres Necios Acusais La Mujer Sin Razon," *nasty men who accuse blame women without reason*; and Argentine-born Alfonsina Storni, 1900 who insisted "Una mano que sabe trabajar, un cerebro que es sano. *A hand that knows how to work, a brain that is healthy… Make your path like the female wolf!*

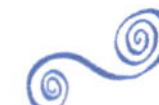

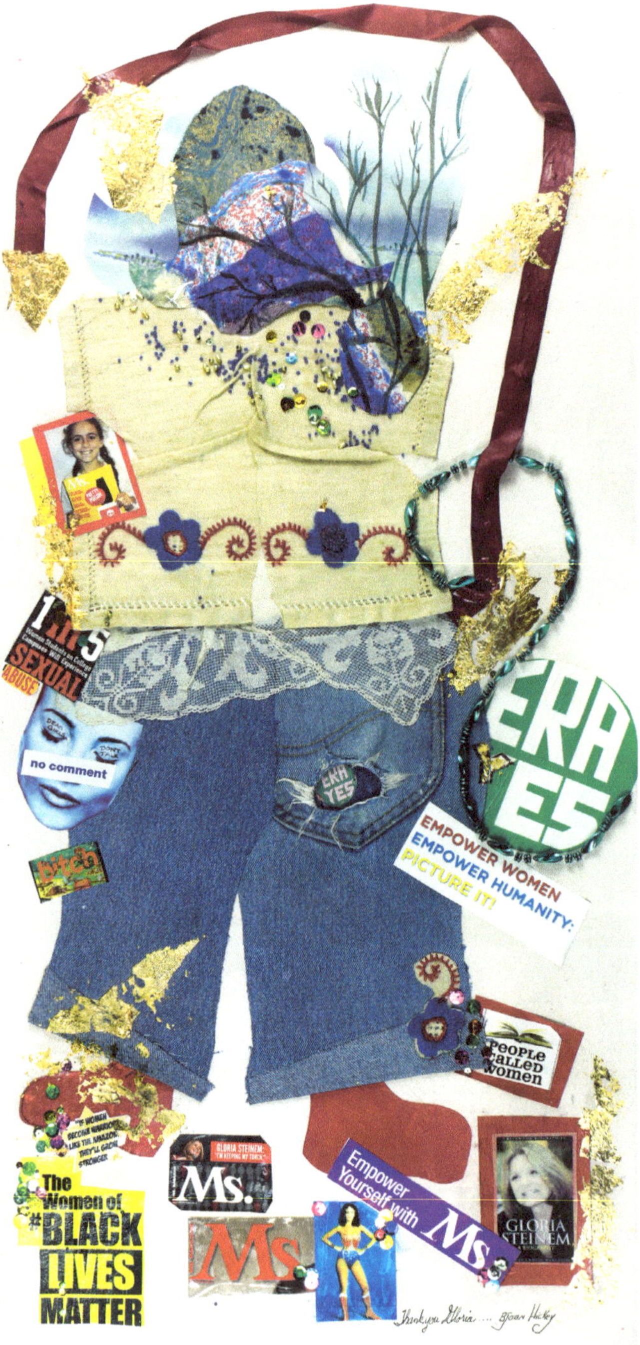

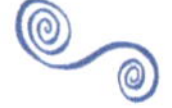

SEXUAL ABUSE
no comment
bitch
ERA ES
ERA YES
EMPOWER WOMEN
EMPOWER HUMANITY.
PICTURE IT!
People Called Women
The Women of #BLACK LIVES MATTER
GLORIA STEINEM: I'M KEEPING MY TORCH
Ms.
Ms
Empower Yourself with Ms
GLORIA STEINEM
Thank you Gloria .... Brian Hickey

THANK YOU, GLORIA STEINEM
(1960 A.D. - Present, 16"w x 24"h)

This icon is a celebration of "People Called Women." As women balancing careers and families from the 1970s to the present, many of us believe in social, economic and political equality for all women and children. Gloria Steinem is a kindred spirit who epitomizes the strong, courageous woman we want our little girls to emulate as they create their own paths in life. The blue jeans are a reference to our little girls. It is women like Gloria who empower us to be our own versions of Wonder Woman: artists, advocates, writers, warriors, guides, goddesses, pioneers, and even Presidents.

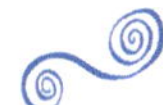

SELECTED BIBLIOGRAPHY

Bahn, Paul. *Cave Art*. Frances Lincoln Limited Publishers: London, 2007.

Barrera, Regina. *Women's Strategic Use of Humor*. Penguin Books: USA, 1991.

Beckett, Wendy. *The Story of Painting*. London: Dorking Kindersley and National Gallery of Art Washington, DC. 1994.

Bolen, M.D. Jean Shinoda. *Goddesses in Every Woman. A New Psychology of Women*. New York: Harper & Row, 1984.

Brown, Nancy Marie. *The Far Traveler, Voyages of a Viking Woman*. New York Houghton Mifflin Harcourt, 2007.

Chicago, Judy. *Embroidering Our Heritage The Dinner Parly Needle Work*. Anchor Books Edition, 1980.

Collins, Gail. *The Amazing Journey of American Women from 1960 to the Present*. New York: Back Bay Books/Little Brown and Company, Hachette Books Group, 2009.

Gadon, Elinor W. *The Once & Future Goddess*. New York: Harper & Row, 1989.

Gilligan, Carol. *In a Different Voice. Psychological Theory and Women's Development*. Cambridge, MA. Harvard University Press. 1992

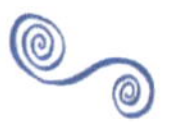

Gombrich E.H. *The Story of Art 10th Edition.* London New York
    Phridon Press, LTD. MCMLX.

Harris, Ann Sutherland, and Linda Nochlin *Women Artists 1550-
    1950.* Los Angeles County Museum of Art, New York: Alfred A.
    Knopf. 1979.

Heilbrun, Carolyn G. *Writing A Woman's Life.* New York. London:
    WW Norton & Company, 1988.

Heller, Nancy G. *Women Artists An Illustrated History.* New York:
    Abbeville Press, 1987.

Jimenez, Juan Ramon. *Platero y Yo 8th Edition.* Madrid. Spain. Aguilar,
    S.A. 1965.

Lippad, Lucy R. *Overlay Contemporary Art and the Art of Prehistory.*
    New York: The New Press, 1983.

Newman, Erich. *The Great Mother an Analysis of the Archetype.* New
    Jersey Princeton University Press, 1955.

Nochlin, Linda. *Women, Art, and Power and Other Essays.* New York:
    Harper & Ron, Publishers, 1988.

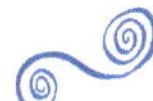

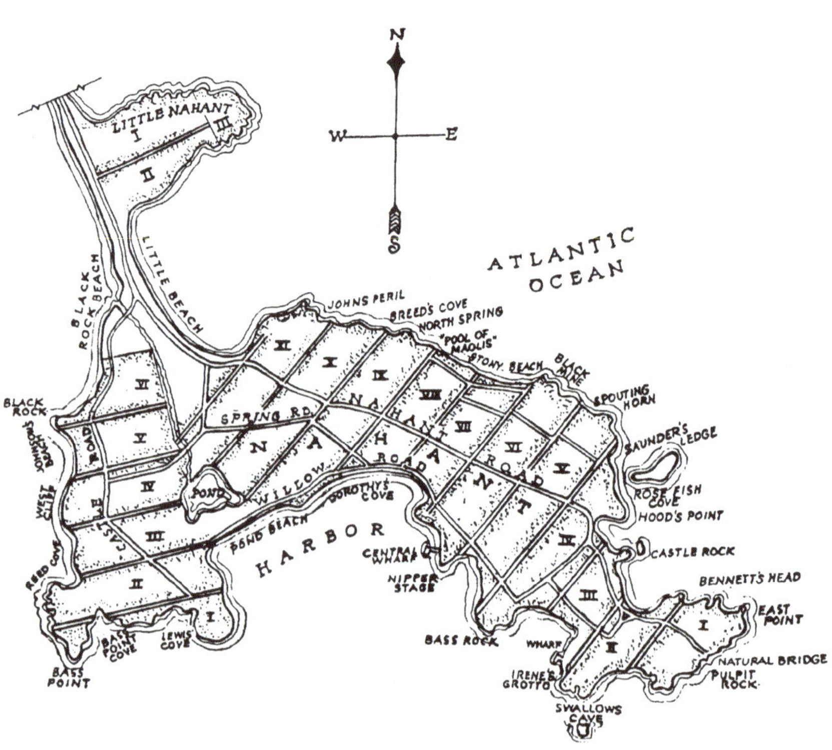

N
W E
S
ATLANTIC OCEAN
LITTLE NAHANT
I III
II
BLACK ROCK BEACH
LITTLE BEACH
JOHNS PERIL
BREED'S COVE
NORTH SPRING
"POOL OF MAOLIS"
STONY BEACH
BLACK MILE
SPOUTING HORN
SAUNDER'S LEDGE
ROSE FISH COVE
HOOD'S POINT
CASTLE ROCK
BENNETT'S HEAD
EAST POINT
NATURAL BRIDGE
PULPIT ROCK
BASS ROCK
WHARF
IRENE'S GROTTO
SWALLOWS COVE
CENTRAL WHARF
NIPPER STAGE
HARBOR
BASS ROCK
LEWIS COVE
BASS POINT COVE
BASS POINT
REED COVE
CASTLE ROAD
WEST CLIFF
JOHNSON'S BEACH
BLACK ROCK
SPRING RD.
WILLOW
DOROTHY'S COVE
POND BEACH
POND
NAHANT ROAD
NAHANT ROAD
ROAD
I
II
III
IV
V
VI
VII
VIII
IX
X
XI

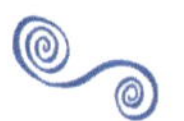

ARTIST STATEMENT OF A NAHANT GIRL

Nahant is a mile long, tiny town due east of Boston, Massachusetts. It extends out into the Atlantic Ocean and is connected to the North Shore by a causeway three miles long. I grew up in a family of seven—Herm and Coey Hussey, Joan, Dave, Leland, Heidi and Hawley—in my great grandmother's home where my family has lived for five generations. We all climbed the rocks, swam in the deep cold green sea, walked everywhere and studied light on water.

The sunrise, the sunset, the moon rises and the seas ravaged by Northeasters were events in our family. My mother and my grandmothers all painted, designed and sewed beautiful clothes for me.

Each of them built sand castles and a lovely welcoming home. Fresh coffee and popovers were a constant treat in the kitchen. All five children and their friends painted, made beautiful things and learned the names of flora and fauna in my mother's art studio. Our father taught math, coached football, and smoked cigars while clamming at our beautiful sandy beach. I wore a tailor-made suit with embroidered initials made by my grandmother to my first teaching position in Bogotá, Colombia. My foremothers had great aspirations for me; after babysitting.

"Shoot for a star, at least you will hit a tree." I live, study light and paint by the sea.

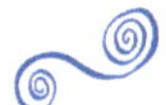

The Myth Redrawn, In The Female Gaze

What do these strong, courageous women through the centuries have to teach us?

30,000 B.C.E.
Cave Women Painting:

#1 "Rock Stars"

Antiquity 2,500 B.C.
Sky altar to:
#2 Optima Principesa
The Great Mother Isis, Aphrodite
#3 The Great Goddess
"Regeneratrix of Thera"

453 - 1329 A.D.
Medieval:
#4 Bridget's Cross
a.k.a.
Bregheta, Celtic Mother of
Healing Fire

1030 - 1066 A.D.
#5 Guidrid the Far Traveler
Wove Sails:
"Women Went a Viking"
Sold Red and Purple Textiles
to Rome

Circa 80 B.C.E. 1550 A.D.
God Gave to Women the Power
to Make Life
#6 Birth Shrine to Eve
Alpha and Omega

1450 - 1550 A.D.
Renaissance:
#7 Madonna, Mother, Warrior
Queen
#8 Medusa's Power

450 B.C.E. - 1660 A.D.
Baroque Painter Artemisia
Gentileschi
#9 Strength, Wisdom, and
Courage: Old Testament, Jewish
Heroine: "Judith Cuts Off the Head
of Holofernes"

1200 - 2000 A.D.
Medieval Chartres:
#10 Persistence, Spirituality, and
Grace from the Black Madonna
(Africa) a.k.a. Artemis

1700 - 1850 A.D.
Vanitas:
#11 Tree of Life
#12 Fève Vulgaire (Ugly Bean)
#13 Intuition
#14 Sacajawea

1900 - 1960 A.D.
#15 Cat and Mouse
#16 Another Nickel Tip
#17 Woman Invents Tiffany Lamp
#18 Alaska: Totem to
Grandmother Fog

Past Into Future
#19 Baubo Figure / Autonomy
#20 Brave Chicago Girls "We
Believe You Anita"
#21 Malala Nobel Prize 2014
Age 17 Shot for Going to School

1960 A.D. - Present
#22 Should a Mother Continue to
Model?
#23 Trading Places (1996)
#24 (La Loba) The Female Wolf
Protect Yourself
#25 Thank You Gloria (Steinem) 2015

9 780692 511275